Jackie

Also edited by
Claire G. Osborne

The Unique Voice of Hillary Rodham Clinton

JACKIE

A Legend Defined

Edited by
CLAIRE G. OSBORNE

AVON BOOKS NEW YORK

AVON BOOKS
A division of
The Hearst Corporation
1350 Avenue of the Americas
New York, New York 10019

Copyright © 1997 by Bill Adler Books
Interior design by Jean Cohn
Front cover photograph by Archive Photos
Published by arrangement with Bill Adler Books
Visit our website at **http://AvonBooks.com**
ISBN: 0-380-79134-X

Library of Congress Cataloging in Publication Data:

Osborne, Claire G.
  Jackie : a legend defined / edited by Claire G. Osborne.
     p.   cm.
Includes bibliographical references.
1. Onassis, Jacqueline Kennedy, 1929–94 — Miscellanea.   2. Celebrities — United States — Biography — Miscellanea.   3. Presidents' spouses — United States — Biography — Miscellanea.   I. Title.
CT275.055205   1997   96-6599
973.922'092 — dc21   CIP
[B]

First Avon Books Trade Printing: July 1997

AVON TRADEMARK REG. U.S. PAT. OFF. AND IN OTHER COUNTRIES, MARCA REGIS-
TRADA, HECHO EN U.S.A.

Printed in the U.S.A.

OPM   10 9 8 7 6 5 4 3 2 1

Contents

Contents

Contents

Jackie

Introduction

Against all her professed wishes, the world's most private woman became the world's most famous. By the time of her death, in 1994, Jacqueline Bouvier Kennedy Onassis had more biographies and periodical articles written on her than any other living woman, yet she had only spoken with a handful of their authors. Somewhere, in the vast forest of Jackie material, past both the inflated iconography and the rumors, assumptions, and outright slanders, lie scattered pieces of fact. This is all we really have of the real Jackie, a series of snapshots—anecdotes, letters, photographs—from which we have built a legend.

The facts in this collection are only pieces of her amazing life, but standing alone, show even more poignantly the drama and subtlety that she gave to the world. One might consider an undertaking like this a book of "trivia," but in the case of Jackie, when most of her life is far beyond the reach of nearly all readers and writers, hardly any piece of evidence about who this woman really was can be considered trivial. This must have been the driving force behind the frenzy at the auction of her estate, where candlesticks and tape measures sold at hundreds of times above their "true" value. Each item is important in maintaining the fractured whole. Each tiny shred of her life is a valuable piece of history.

Jackie

— JACKIE AS A YOUNG GIRL —

I

Heritage and Childhood

Ancestry

Jackie's great-great-grandfather on her father's side was Michel Bouvier, a cabinetmaker who came to the United States around 1815 and settled in Philadelphia. He became wealthy by manufacturing marble and veneer tabletops and investing the money in real estate. His daughter raised the family's social status when she married a Drexel, and her sons entered the New York Stock Exchange. It was through this connection that the Bouviers were later linked with the Vanderbilts, the Morgans, and the Harrimans in business ventures.

Her grandfather on her father's side, John Vernou Bouvier, Jr., or "the Major," was a well-respected lawyer who retired from law to join his uncle in his stock brokerage, and eventually inherited much of his uncle's estate. To improve his social standing, he fabricated a genealogy, *Our Forebearers*, to include French aristocracy, among them a member of the French Parliament, as well as a coat of arms. He also claimed there was a close friendship between Joseph Bonaparte and Michel Bouvier. In actuality, Bonaparte had contracted Bouvier for carpentry and construction work.

The family's true ancestry is Francois Bouvier, an ironmonger whose wife was a maid. John Bouvier's genealogy makes reference to a nobleman of the same name, but he lived a full two centuries earlier.

Jackie was unaware of her true roots until the genealogy was closely examined by historians after she became First Lady.

Bouvier is French for ox driver or cowherd.

Her grandfather on her mother's side, James T. Lee, was a well-known and prolific developer who had a long list of Manhattan buildings to his credit, including 740 Park Avenue, which would become one of Jackie's childhood homes.

After graduating from Columbia Law School in 1899 and starting his own practice, he worked for real estate developers and learned enough to enter the profession with a partner in 1908. Among his developments that still stand are 998 Fifth Avenue, one of Manhattan's most luxurious and exclusive apartment houses, and the Shelton Hotel, now the Marriott East Side Hotel, at Forty-ninth Street and Lexington. When it was completed in 1923, it was the tallest hotel in the world. The *New York Times* estimated his total developments to be worth $35 million in 1923.

This heritage may explain Jackie's love of old buildings, as well as her passionate campaigns to preserve Manhattan's architectural heritage.

Parents

Jackie's mother, Janet Norton Lee, described herself as "one of the Lees of Maryland," but her grandparents were actually Irish immigrants who had come to America to escape the potato famine.

She grew up wealthy, attending Miss Spence's School, making her debut at Sherry's, and attending Sweet Briar College and Barnard.

Jackie's father, John Vernou Bouvier III, went by the name Jack Bouvier and was widely known as Black Jack, a nickname that came from his dark tan as much as from his reputation as a gambler and womanizer. He was thirty-eight when Jackie was born.

He graduated from Yale in 1914 near the bottom

of his class. He enlisted with the U.S. Army in 1917 but, according to his letters, did not serve with distinction, fighting his "toughest battles in the smoke-filled, honky-tonk back-alleys and brothels of North and South Carolina, waiting for this dirty little war to end."

He acquired a seat on the New York Stock Exchange in 1922 with loans from his family. He did well, earning over $75,000 per year, but was reckless with his money.

Jack Bouvier met Janet Lee when she was in her early teens in East Hampton. They were engaged in spring of 1928 and married on July 7, 1928.

Janet Lee Bouvier was twenty-two when she delivered Jackie the following year, on July 28, 1929.

Jack Bouvier began to have trouble with his investments when Franklin D. Roosevelt established the Securities Exchange Commission, which outlawed many of his best moneymaking schemes. He placed blame for his misfortunes on the head of the SEC, who was none other than Joseph P. Kennedy, father of Jackie's future husband.

Due to Jack's wild and often indiscreet infidelities, he and Janet began a six-month trial separation on September 30, 1936, at her insistence. She received temporary custody of the children, and $1,050 per month for their support. Jackie was seven.

The two were reconciled in 1937, due mostly to Jack's efforts. Although Janet was skeptical, she rejoined Jack for the sake of the children. By September they separated again, now calling it "permanent." After some meager attempts at further reconciliation on Jack's part, Janet finally sued for divorce and took her story to the press.

The final divorce called for Jack to provide Janet with $1,000 per month for alimony and child support. He was also charged with covering "all necessary medical, surgical and dental expenses and the school tuition for each of the children during their respective minorities." He was permitted visitation rights on alternate Saturdays and Sundays, one day during the week, half of winter and spring breaks, and six weeks during the summer. Jackie was ten when the divorce was finalized.

Janet started dating investment banker Hugh Dudley Auchincloss, Jr., in 1941. He had been twice married and had three children. In 1942 he was assigned to a planning unit in Kingston, Jamaica, by the Office of Naval Intelligence. He married Janet in a spur-of-the-moment ceremony the day he left for Jamaica.

Jackie called her stepfather Uncle Hughdie.

Janet Auchincloss, Jr., daughter of Janet and Hugh, was born in 1945, and Jamie Auchincloss was born two years later. This brought the total number of children in the Auchincloss household to seven.

Jackie's father had meanwhile taken up house with a married Englishwoman, who gave birth to twins she claimed were Jack's. They were raised by the woman and her husband in England, and while Jack never met them, Jackie visited them in 1949. Their relation to Jackie was kept secret until it was revealed in *The Kennedys: Dynasty and Disaster*, by John Davis, published in 1984. By that time, both were dead.

Black Jack died in 1957 from liver cancer at the age of sixty-six. Jackie attempted to see him one last time as he lay in a coma, but he died before she arrived at the hospital. A nurse at his bedside claims his final word was "Jackie."

Jackie wrote his obituary and had Jack present it to the *New York Times*, hoping his reputation would ensure prominent publication. She then took responsibility for funeral arrangements, which took place at St. Patrick's Cathedral. She had the cathedral adorned with daisies in white wicker baskets. "I want everything to look like a summer garden."

She kissed his coffin and placed in it a gold bracelet he had given her as a graduation present from Vassar. She did not cry at the funeral.

Jackie inherited $80,000, after taxes, from her father. Her sister Lee had received roughly the same amount.

Jackie as a Child

Jackie was born Jacqueline Lee Bouvier on July 28, 1929, in a Southampton hospital in New York. She was named in honor of her father, Jack Bouvier.

Jackie's family took up residence in an eleven-room duplex at 740 Park Avenue in Manhattan. The building was owned by Janet's father.

The family also rented a summerhouse at 111 Egypt Lane in East Hampton. Jackie's second birthday party was held there, and shortly afterward her name appeared in print, in *The East Hampton Star*, for the first time: "Little Jackie Bouvier, daughter of Jack Bouvier and the former Janet Lee, will not make her bow to society for another sixteen years or more, but she was a charming hostess at her second birthday party given at the home of her parents, 'Rowdy Hall' on Egypt Lane. The party featured games and pony rides for the children, followed by Jack Horner pie and birthday cake."

Within a month, she was again mentioned in *The Star*. The occasion was a pet show.

As a child, she preferred the name Jacqueline, but everyone still called her Jackie.

Jackie's sister, Caroline Lee Bouvier, was born on March 3, 1933. She said of her sister, "Nothing could ever come between us," and "Lee was always the pretty one. I guess I was supposed to be the smart one."

In the same year, while Jackie was walking with her nanny and sister in Central Park, she became separated from them. When she was approached by a police officer, she said in a stern, concerned voice, "My nurse and baby sister seem to be lost."

Jackie's favorite playmates were her cousins Scotty and Shella Bouvier. They established a club known as "The Blood Brothers," complete with clubhouse.

The Bouviers later used Jack's father's house in East Hampton, known as Wildmoor, as their summer home.

After her mother remarried, the family lived between Hugh's homes in Merrywood, Virginia, and his ancestral home, Hammersmith Farm, in Newport. The Merrywood home was a Georgian-style mansion with forty-six acres of land across the Potomac from Washington. There was an Olympic-sized swimming pool, indoor badminton court, two stables, a four-car garage, eight bedrooms, a dining room that could accommodate over three hundred guests, and separate quarters for the servants.

After moving to the Merrywood, Virginia, mansion, Janet gleefully took to redecorating, reclaiming the interior from Hugh's former wives, with much of the same enthusiasm and taste that Jackie exhibited during her restoration of the White House.

Jackie's bedroom at Merrywood was across from the former bedroom of Gore Vidal, son of Nina Gore Vidal, Hugh's second wife. Gore (then known as Eugene Vidal) had left Merrywood before Jackie arrived, and she did not meet the writer until 1949. For riding wear she often wore the dress shirts that he had left behind.

Hammersmith Farm was a twenty-eight-room mansion with thirteen fireplaces, a wraparound terrace, and an elevator. Overlooking Narragansett Bay, the grounds covered ninety-seven acres, with stables for horses and barns for bulls and Hugh's Black Angus cows. After seeing that the downstairs rooms had white walls and plush red carpet, Jackie suggested that all future family dogs be black to match. Her suggestion was followed.

Due to the war effort, Hammersmith Farm was both short on labor (it had formerly been tended by sixteen house servants and thirty-two groundskeepers and farmhands) and needed by the local naval base for milk and eggs. Janet assigned chores to her children, and Jackie's primary duty for the summer of 1943 was to feed the farm's two thousand chickens.

II

Education and Early Socializing

Activities and Influences

Before entering kindergarten, Jackie read *The Wizard of Oz*, *Little Lord Fauntleroy*, and *Winnie the Pooh*.

She first read Chekhov at the age of six. When her mother asked her if she understood all the words, she said, "Yes, except what's a midwife?" At age eleven, her favorite books were *Gone with the Wind* and the works of Lord Byron.

At ten years old, Jackie memorized "The Vision of Sir Launfal," by James Russell Lowell, to surprise her mother for her birthday. The poem was eleven pages long.

Jackie performed even greater feats of memory later in life. For a lecture class on Shakespeare at Vassar, Jackie memorized the entire text of *Antony and Cleopatra*. And early in her marriage to Jack, she committed one of his favorite poems, *John Brown's Body*, to memory so she could recite it to him.

Encouraged by her aunt Edith, Jackie began to write poems and short stories at the age of eight and decorated her manuscripts with simple line drawings. Her early poems were on the topic of nature, while her short stories dealt with the family pets. One of these, "The Adventures of George Woofty, Esq.," detailed her pet terrier's fictional romance with Caprice, a female Bouvier des Flandres.

Once, in 1936, Jack took Jackie and her sister to the Stock Exchange. The entire floor knew who they were, and applauded. They performed curtsies, and the traders applauded again.

Other childhood activities included ballet lessons and painting.

Jackie's Poetry
Christmas

> Christmas is coming
> Santa Claus is near
> Reindeer hooves will soon be drumming
> On the rooftops loud and clear
> The shops are filled with people

Snow is coming down
And everyone is merry
In such a busy town.

—at age eight

When I go down by the sandy shore
I can think if nothing I want more
Than to live by the blooming blue sea
As the seagulls flutter round about me.

—at age ten

Poem to commemorate the birth of her half sister Janet Auchincloss:

Listen, my children, and you shall hear,
It was nineteen hundred and forty-five
When Janet Jennings became alive.
She made all the headlines far and near
And became the Baby of the Year!
Crowds to do her homage came,
Bringing priceless gifts and rare
The flower shop all had a boom
And Western Union tore its hair.

—at age fifteen

19

A poem written for her father:
>   I love walking on the angry shore
>   To watch the angry sea
>   Where summer people were before,
>   And now there's only me.

Excerpt from a poem written for Jack during their honeymoon:
>   He will build empires
>   And he will have sons
>   Others break down
>   When he pursues his course
>   He will find love
>   Without finding peace
>   For it is necessary to search for
>   The Golden Fleece
>   And all that waits for him
>   Is the sea and the wind.

Jack tried to get Jackie to publish this poem, but she refused.

Schools

Jackie attended kindergarten at Miss Yates' nursery school, and Chapin School for elementary school.

20

The headmistress at Chapin told Jackie's mother that the young girl had "the most inquiring mind we've seen in years." However, Jackie rebelled against the regimentation of the school, and was frequently bored in class. A classmate of Jackie's reported to her mother that she was "the very worst behaved girl in school." Her antics included dipping other girls' braids in her inkwell and dropping water bombs from a perch on the hallway lockers.

When her mother asked what happened when she was sent to the headmistress's office, Jackie replied, "Well, I go to the office and Miss Stringfellow says, 'Jacqueline, sit down. I've heard bad reports about you.' I sit down. Then Miss Stringfellow says a lot of things, but I don't listen."

After relocating to Merrywood, Jackie attended Holton-Arms, then in downtown Washington. It was here that she discovered her love for languages. "Although I hated to admit it, I adored Latin."

In 1944, after two years at Holton-Arms, Jackie went to boarding school at Miss Porter's School in Farmington, Connecticut, founded in 1843. The conditions at the all-girls school were strict: no card playing, Friday afternoon tea with the teachers, no reading of romance novels, no permission to leave the school grounds without special arrangement.

While at Miss Porter's (known to its 150 students simply as "Farmington"), Jackie was on a $50-per-month allowance from her father, an amount that would be sure to keep her something of an outcast from her extremely well cared for classmates.

Jackie was a staff member of the Farmington student paper, *Salmagundy*, which printed her drawings and poems, and an actress with "The Farmington Players," which produced two plays per year. She performed the role of Mr. Bingsley in a stage adaptation of *Pride and Prejudice* in her junior year.

Jackie maintained an A average at Farmington. When she graduated in 1947, she claimed in her yearbook entry that her ambition in life was "not to be a housewife."

The following fall, Jackie enrolled at Vassar College. By 1948 she expressed discontent with the school, calling it "that goddamn Vassar." She exceeded in her studies, making the dean's list and receiving straight A's.

Jackie was accepted to the Junior Year Abroad program and chose the Sorbonne as her destination. After spending six weeks in intensive language study, she rented a room from Countess Guyot de Renty at 78 Avenue Mozart. Jackie had known the countess's daughter, Claude de Renty, from the States.

After her junior year in Paris, Jackie transferred her college credits to George Washington University in Washington, D.C., and graduated as a French literature major.

Religion

Jackie was baptized on December 22, 1929, at the Church of St. Ignatius Loyola in New York. Janet asked her father to be godfather to Jackie, but he was late to the ceremony, so the role was filled by Miche Bouvier, Jackie's nine-year-old cousin.

St. Ignatius was also the church of her christening, confirmation, and funeral mass.

It was important to Jackie to give Caroline a Catholic education, especially after the death of Patrick. When Caroline was six, she sent her to Georgetown Visitation Academy, a convent in Washington. On the first day of class, Jackie asked if she could sit in. Caroline's instructor, Sister Joanne, asked the class to think about creation and then draw a picture of it with crayons.

While other pupils drew animals, plants, and Adam

23

and Eve, Caroline's picture was solid black. Worries about vast existential despair manifesting itself in tiny Caroline briefly visited Sister Joanne and Jackie, but when the instructor asked the children to explain their drawings, Caroline said, "In the beginning there was nothing but darkness, but then God put a light up in the sky." They could then see that Caroline had allowed for stars and a moon in her interpretation.

Jackie told Sister Joanne after class, "If I had had religion taught to me in that way, it would have been a much happier experience for me."

After the shooting of Bobby Kennedy, Jackie reflected on the role of Catholicism while waiting in the hospital:

> The Church is . . . at its best only at the time of death. The rest of the time it's often rather silly little men running around in their black suits. But the Catholic Church understands death. I'll tell you who else understands death are the black churches. I remember at the funeral of Martin Luther King, I was looking at those faces, and I realized that they knew death. They see it all the time and they're ready for it . . . in the way in which a good Catholic

is. We know death. . . . As a matter of fact, if it weren't for the children, we'd welcome it.

Knowledge and Skills

Jackie was one year old when her mother first placed her on a pony, setting in motion a lifelong love of riding. She competed in the Long Island horse-show circuit from the age of five. Her first horse, Danseuse, a chestnut show horse, was given to her by her mother as a birthday present.

She captured a double victory in the junior horsemanship competition at the Madison Square Garden National Championships in 1941.

Jackie was fluent in Italian, French, and Spanish.

In Venice during her 1951 trip to Europe, Jackie took private drawing lessons from a young Italian artist.

She was a tournament Scrabble player, known as one of the best in the country. After marrying Jack, she took up bridge, learning from advanced players in Washington. She also tried her hand at golf to be able to play with her husband.

Clubs and Societies

Jackie won first prize in the East Hampton Riding Club's costume class with an American Indian costume she designed herself.

Jackie's stepfather was a member of the top clubs in areas surrounding Washington, Hammersmith, and New York, including Bailey's Beach, the Newport Country Club, the Metropolitan Club, the Chevy Chase Country Club, and the Knickerbocker Club in New York.

At her mother's insistence, Jackie attended dance and etiquette classes with Mrs. Shippen, well known in local social circles, in Washington, D.C. Shippen also gave dance parties for her students during vacations.

Jackie would say later: "I was a tomboy. I decided to learn to dance and I became feminine."

Jackie the Debutante

Jackie initiated her own coming-out party, asking her stepfather if she could debut at Hammersmith Farm. Jackie's mother arranged it as an afternoon tea for three hundred guests, and held it on the same day that Jamie Auchincloss was christened.

The next phase of her coming out was a formal

26

dinner and dance at the Clambake Club in Newport. Jackie's frock was called by the society pages "a designer's dream" and "a lovely white tulle gown with an off-the-shoulder neckline and bouffant skirt." Jackie admitted much later that it was off-the-rack from a New York department store, costing less than sixty dollars.

Hearst gossip columnist Igor Cassini dubbed Jackie "Queen of the Debutantes" in 1947. He wrote:

> The Queen of the Year for 1947 is Jacqueline Bouvier, a regal brunette who has classic features and the daintiness of Dresden porcelain. She has poise, is soft-spoken and intelligent, everything the leading debutante should be. Her background is strictly "Old Guard." . . . Jacqueline is now studying at Vassar. You don't have to read a batch of press clippings to be aware of her qualities.

Igor Cassini is the brother of Oleg Cassini, who would become Jackie's personal fashion designer during the White House years.

On weekends from Vassar, Jackie attended debutante functions at places like Glen Cove, Rye, and Greenwich, Connecticut.

Jackie spent July and August of 1948 on a tour of Europe with her friends Helen and Judy Bowdoin, stepdaughters of Undersecretary of the Treasury Edward F. Foley, and Julia Bissell, a friend from Baltimore. They were chaperoned by Jackie's beloved former Latin teacher from Holton-Arms. The group attended a Royal Garden Party at Buckingham Palace and were greeted by King George VI, Queen Elizabeth, and Sir Winston Churchill in a reception line.

Jackie briefly entertained the idea of becoming a fashion model in 1948. She modeled in amateur benefit shows in Newport and East Hampton, and was paid a nominal fee by *Life* for an appearance in a Vassar College show.

In 1951 Jackie won *Vogue*'s Prix de Paris, a writing and design contest for which contestants submit four papers on fashion, a personal profile, plans for an issue of *Vogue*, and an essay on the topic of "People I Wish I Had Known," Jackie selected Sergei Diaghilev, Charles Baudelaire, and Oscar Wilde as the people she wished she had known:

Baudelaire and Wilde were both rich men's sons who lived like dandies, ran through what they had, and died in extreme poverty. Both were poets and idealists who could paint sinfulness with honesty and still believe in something higher—Diaghileff [sic] possessed what is rarer than artistic genius in any one field, the sensitivity to take the best of each man and incorporate it into a masterpiece all the more precious because it lives only in the minds of those who have seen it and disintegrates as soon as he is gone.

And for her self-portrait essay:

Being away from home gave me a chance to look at myself with a jaundiced eye. I learned not to be ashamed of a real hunger for knowledge, something I had always tried to hide, and I came home glad to start in here again but with a love for Europe that I am afraid will never leave me.

Jackie was singled out from 1,280 contestants for the prize, a one-year trainee position with *Vogue*, six

29

months in the Paris offices and six months in New York.

Jackie's mother and stepfather, however, convinced Jackie to not accept the reward, feeling that she had already spent too much time away from home. They agreed, however, to send her on another trip to Europe with her sister Lee.

Jackie's First Job

In December 1951 Jackie interviewed for a position at the *Times-Herald*, a now defunct Washington newspaper, then located at Thirteenth and H streets. The interview was arranged by a friend of her stepfather.

Within weeks Jackie had moved from being a gofer to city room receptionist. A position opened when a columnist resigned and the paper decided to fill the space with an "inquiring photographer" feature, and Jackie volunteered for the post.

Her duties were to do interviews, with both known figures and the "man on the street," and accompany the story with a photograph. She mostly devised her own questions, such as "Do the rich enjoy life more than the poor?" "What do you think women desire most?" "Would you like to crash high society?" and others that seemed to strangely foreshadow Jackie's life: "What prominent person's death affected you most?" "Should a candidate's wife campaign with her husband?" "Would you like your son to grow up to be president?" "Which first lady would you most like to have been?"

Jackie interviewed then Vice President Richard Nixon's six-year-old daughter in 1952, asking what she thought of her father's new post. "He's always away. If he's famous, why can't he stay at home?" she answered.

From these assignments, Jackie soon received by-lines and a raise from $42.50 to $56.75 per week.

Although she claimed she knew how to use a camera in order to get the position, she quickly took a class in news photography. She used a large, professional Speed Graflex for her shoots.

Early Romances

While in boarding school, Jackie did not date frequently, in the words of one classmate, preferring books to boys. When she did date, it was with small groups, and always with boys whose parents were friendly with her parents.

She started dating frequently while at Vassar, but

31

according to her classmates, never spoke of her dates or engaged in gossip. Years later she referred to her college dates as "beetle-browed bores" and insisted she could never marry any of them, "not because of them, but because of their lives." Some said she took dating as an opportunity to improve her social skills.

One of her frequent dates told of how she avoided sexual encounters: "There was a ridiculous rumor going around that I'd bedded down with her. I wish it were true. But it wasn't. You couldn't get to first base with Jackie." Said another, "You were lucky to get a peck on the cheek."

In 1948 Jackie would often go dancing with Colonel Serge Obolensky, a White Russian prince who was then over sixty years old. She was admonished for this choice by her father.

In Paris Jackie met Ormande de Kay, and allowed him to escort her around Paris. "We did all the usual and expected things that young couples do in Paris—traveled by Metro, queued up at the neighborhood cinema, walked hand in hand along the Seine. . . ."

They met again at a party in Washington to celebrate the two hundredth anniversary of Georgetown, and Ormande, then on active duty in the navy, would hitchhike from Charleston to visit her at Merrywood.

Jackie also dated writer John Phillips Marquand, Jr., in Paris. According to Gore Vidal, who knew Marquand well, it was with him that Jackie lost her virginity, after a night out, in a stalled lift on the way up to his apartment. He purports Jackie said afterward: "Oh! Is that all there is to it?" Vidal added that they continued to have "a very passionate affair." Marquand, Jr., who was then working on his first novel, *The Second Happiest day*, denies all this emphatically. "It's bullshit, totally apocryphal, categorically untrue." He blames the Kitty Kelley biography, *Jackie Oh!* for starting and perpetuating the rumor.

Jackie met John Husted, who worked as an investment banker after serving with the American Field Service during World War II, through a friend of her stepsister Yusha Auchincloss in 1951. John and Hugh's fathers had been friends at Yale. Shortly after meeting, John proposed to Jackie, first over the phone and then at The Polo Bar in the Westbury Hotel, New York. She accepted. Hugh threw an engagement party at Merrywood, and John gave Jackie a diamond and sapphire ring that had belonged to his mother.

In January 1952 Jackie wrote to Ormande de Kay, then serving in Korea, to let him know that their romance had come to an end. "I want you to be the first to know that I've found the love of my life, the man I want to marry." The letter was delayed in reaching him, and by the time he did get it, Jackie had broken her engagement with John Husted and was nearly engaged to Jack.

While working at the *Times-Herald,* Jackie would spend weekends with John Husted in New York. Sometimes he would visit her at Merrywood, or they would meet at his parents' house in Bedford, Connecticut. Still, John described their relationship as "chaste."

In March of 1952, Jackie's mother found, through a few inquiries, that John made only $17,000 per year and expressed concern about his being able to support Jackie. It was around this time that Jackie, although still engaged, began to date other men, including a former *Times-Herald* feature writer who was then at the State Department, an air force pilot, and a *Time* correspondent who was a paratrooper in World War II.

Her supervisor at the *Times-Herald* asked her once what her ideal man would be. She responded: "I look at a male model and am bored in three minutes. I like men with funny noses, ears that protrude, irregular teeth, short men, skinny men, fat men. Above all, he must have a keen mind." In a dinner conversation she added, "He must weigh more and have bigger feet than I do."

Jackie met Charles Bartlett in 1948, when he was with the *Chattanooga Times*. He held some interest in Jackie himself, but claims he nearly introduced her to John F. Kennedy at his brother's wedding in East Hampton. However, she became involved in conversation with former prizefighter Gene Tunney, while John was talking about politics at the other side of the room.

III

Marriage and Children

Meeting Kennedy

There are a few different accounts of the meeting in May 1951 of Jackie and John F. Kennedy, who was then U.S. representative from the Eleventh Congressional District of Massachusetts. Charles Bartlett maintains that he introduced the two, saying that he knew Kennedy's taste in women, and Jackie was one he could appreciate. Others say that it was his wife, Martha, who introduced them because Charles was still carrying a torch for Jackie, taking her out for lunch and then bringing her home for dinner. In this account, Martha arranged a dinner party of several available single men and women, placed Jack and Jackie on a couch, served them drinks, and left them alone.

Kennedy himself recalled in a *Time* interview that

he was drawn to Jackie during the party for her intelligence and sense of purpose. "So I leaned over the table and asked her for a date." Jackie replied that asparagus wasn't on the menu.

Charles Bartlett maintains that while the two were walking out to their cars, Jack asked Jackie if she wanted to go out for a late-night drink, when one of Jackie's ex-boyfriends who had passed by the Bartletts' was discovered in her backseat. He had seen her car and thought this a good practical joke. Jack excused himself, caught off guard and flustered.

Jackie's comment on the matter was: "I met him at the home of friends of ours who had been shamelessly matchmaking for a year, and usually that doesn't work out, but this time it did, so I am very grateful to them."

The two didn't meet again until winter of 1951, and Jackie was still engaged to John Husted. This time Jackie invited Kennedy to be her escort to another dinner party at the Bartletts'. Their first date was shortly afterward, when Jack took her dancing at the Shoreham Hotel.

Jackie confided to a friend that she was attracted to Jack because he was "dangerous, just like Black Jack."

Courtship

Jack was preparing for a Senate race, so their dating during that time was, according to Jackie, "spasmodic." "He'd call me from some oyster bar up on the Cape with a great clinking of coins, to ask me out to the movies the following Wednesday." However, Jack was in Washington from Tuesday to Thursday of each week, and they usually saw each other then. She also visited him in his Boston apartment/campaign office.

The couple saw each other much more frequently by April 1952, typically joining friends for dinner or board games. Some of their company at this time were Senator and Mrs. Albert Gore, Senator and Mrs. John Sherman Cooper, Jeff and Pat Roche, and Robert and Ethel Kennedy.

Jack's close friend Lem Billings describes their courtship as passionate: "There were those evenings when they would simply neck in the backseat of Jack's car." In an interview he described one incident of being discovered on a side street by a state trooper: "The trooper drove up, climbed out of his patrol car, and shined his flashlight into the backseat of Jack's convertible. By this time Jack had managed to take off Jackie's brassiere. Apparently the trooper recognized Jack, because he apologized and retreated."

However, Jackie had still not broken her engagement to John Husted. She finally did so in March 1952. She slipped his engagement ring in his pocket as they drove to the airport.

In summer of 1952 she first met the Kennedy clan in Hyannis Port. She did not initially hit it off with the Kennedy girls, Eunice, Jean, and Pat, and didn't fit in with their constant activity and gamesmanship. She referred to them as the "Rah-Rah Girls," while they, seeing Jackie as diminutive and quiet in comparison, referred to her as "the Debutante." Jackie at first made attempts to join in their frequent touch football games, but gave up within a year after the wedding when a Harvard classmate of Ted Kennedy's fell on her and broke her ankle.

However, she was extremely well liked by Jack's father, Joe Kennedy. "Joe Kennedy not only condoned the marriage, he ordained it," said family friend and close confidant of Jack's, Lem Billings.

In November 1952 she informed her cousin John Davis of the relationship but played it down, saying, "The Kennedys are really terrible bourgeois," and complaining of Jack's allergies: "Imagine me with someone allergic to horses!"

She also confided to a friend of her mother's that

she felt Jack would have "a profound, perhaps disturbing, influence upon her." She also knew at this time that he was not particularly inclined toward marriage.

Hearing that Jack frequently ate lunches from a paper bag at his Senate office desk, Jackie would bring him hot lunches for two. Knowing that he followed her column, she would needle him by asking her interview subjects questions such as "Do you think the Irish are deficient in the art of love?"

Jack escorted Jackie to the Eisenhower Inaugural Ball in January 1953. Jackie covered the ball for the *Times-Herald*, and this, along with the fact that she cohosted a cocktail party with Jack that evening, nearly brought their relationship into full public view.

Jackie interviewed Jack in his Senate offices on April 19, 1953, asking him the loaded question: "Can you give any reason why a contented bachelor would want to get married?" The publication of the interview brought them even closer to going public with their relationship.

As with their initial meeting, there are different accounts of Jack's marriage proposal. One has Jack proposing shortly after Jackie's sister's wedding in April 1953, saying that he had known for a year that she was "the one," but had wanted to wait. "How big of you," she retorted.

Another account pushes the proposal back one month, while Jackie was in London covering the coronation of Queen Elizabeth for the *Times-Herald* in May 1953. After he sent her a telegram—ARTICLES EXCELLENT BUT YOU ARE MISSED—they talked on the phone, and he proposed.

In either case, Jackie did not give an immediate answer, concerned about losing her independence, Jack's own fierce independence, and their twelve-year age difference.

Jack's low commitment to true romance may have also been a question. Prior to the telegram, the only other piece of courtship correspondence she received from Jack was a postcard from Bermuda that read "Wish you were here. Cheers, Jack."

According to Gore Vidal, Jackie made a side trip to Paris, where she rekindled her affair with John Marquand, Jr., but informed him as she was preparing to leave that she intended to marry Jack. Marquand, Jr., denies this affair as well, although acknowledged that he saw her in Paris and that she mentioned the proposal.

Jackie sat next to Zsa Zsa Gabor on the plane

back to Washington, and interrogated her about cosmetics. As they were getting off the plane, Gabor recognized Jack, whom she knew from when he was a U.S. representative. (It had been supposed that they were intimate.) She admonished Jack: "She's a lovely girl, don't dare corrupt her." Jackie replied, "He already has."

She remarked to a friend during their courtship, "I'm the luckiest girl in the world. Mummy is terrified of Jack because she can't push him around at all."

Jackie told some of her family about the engagement, but asked them to keep it to themselves, as *The Saturday Evening Post* was preparing to run an article on Jack, "The Senate's Gay Young Bachelor."

The engagement was announced on June 23, 1953, and was reported in newspapers across the country. One reporter asked her what they had in common, and Jackie answered: "Since Jack is such a violently independent person, and I, too, am so independent, this relationship will take a lot of working out."

A *Life* photographer spent three days with the couple, snapping hundreds of shots for a cover story on their budding romance. Jackie was informed by Jack's sisters that this publicity was necessary for Jack's career.

Jack gave Jackie a two-carat, twinned, square-cut diamond and emerald engagement ring, purchased from Van Cleef & Arpels, the famed New York jeweler.

The couple attended two engagement parties, one thrown by Janet and Hugh Auchincloss at Hammersmith Farm, the other by friends of the Kennedys, the Harringtons, on the edge of the Hyannis Port Golf Club.

The night before the ceremony the bridal dinner was held at the Clambake Club, where Jackie's coming-out party had been held. The fourteen ushers received Brooks Brothers umbrellas, and the ten bridesmaids were given monogrammed silver picture frames.

The Wedding

Jack and Jackie were married on September 12, 1953, at St. Mary's Church in Newport, Rhode Island. Jackie was twenty-four and Jack was thirty-six.

Seven hundred guests were at the wedding, and an additional six hundred came to the reception.

The ceremony was performed by Richard Cardinal Cushing, archbishop of Boston, who was assisted by the Very Reverend John J. Cavanaugh, past president

44

of Notre Dame, and the Very Reverend James Kellor of New York. Tenor Luigi Vena performed "Ave Maria" and "Jesu, Amor Mi." Cushing conferred an apostolic blessing on the couple from Pope Pius XII.

Jackie's sister Lee was matron of honor and along with the eleven bridesmaids, wore pink taffeta dresses with satin sashes and bandeaux for their hair. Jackie's half sister was flower girl, and her half brother was page boy. Bobby Kennedy was best man.

Jackie's father, suffering from one of his now frequent drinking binges, failed to appear at the wedding. The role of giving Jackie away was taken up by her stepfather at the last minute. However, a friend of Jack's, acting on his request, managed to slip him into the church during the ceremony.

While Janet and the Auchinclosses were coping with the change of plans, Jack played touch football with his brothers and the usher. A few scratches on his face from the game were touched up in the wedding photos.

A crowd of three thousand spectators gathered outside police barricades surrounding the church.

Jackie's dress was designed around her grandmother's rose-point lace veil. The veil was yellow from age, so her dress was ivory to match, rather than the

traditional white. Made from over fifty yards of material, it featured an off-the-shoulder neckline, cap
sleeves, a tight waist, and flourishes down to the
ground. The veil was worn as a back-of-the-head cap
adorned with orange blossoms and trailed behind her.

The dress was described by one journalist as "atro-
cious," and was not Jackie's preference. Janet had the
dress designed by Ann Lowe, in Jackie's words, a
"colored woman dressmaker" whose dresses were
somewhat known among high society. The original
dress had been destroyed by floods five days before
the wedding, but Lowe managed to bring the piece
together in that short time. She appeared at the wedding to hold Jackie's veil.

Her bridal bouquet was composed of pink and
white orchids, stephanotis, and gardenias. At the reception it was caught by Nancy Tuckerman, who became one of Jackie's closest friends.

The *New York Times* said the wedding "far sur-
passed the Astor-French wedding of 1943."

The reception was held at Hammersmith Farm.
Jack and Jackie were in the reception line for three
and a half hours to greet the thirteen hundred guests.

One glitch at the reception was the caterer accidentally bringing the Moët Vintage to the "help," includ-

ing over five hundred chauffeurs, gathered under a tent by themselves, while the guests were served cheaper champagne.

Music was provided by Meyer Davis, who had performed at the wedding of Jackie's parents. Jack requested "I Married an Angel" for his first dance with Jackie.

The wedding cake, gift of a baker from Quincy, Massachusetts, was five-tiered and four feet high.

Jack's wedding present to Jackie was a $10,000 diamond bracelet, and Joe Kennedy's gift to Jackie was a large diamond pin. There were two truckloads of wedding presents from the guests.

Before leaving for the honeymoon, Jackie changed into a tailored gray Chanel suit and wore the diamond pin from Joe Kennedy.

The newlyweds took a limousine to a local airport, flew to New York by private plane, spent two days at the Waldorf-Astoria, and then went on to Acapulco. They stayed in a prominent pink villa perched on a cliff overlooking the Pacific. Jackie had seen the villa on her first trip to Mexico, and mentioned it in passing while the wedding was being planned. It happened that the villa was owned by Don Miguel Alemán, President of Mexico and old friend of Joe Kennedy, who surprised his daughter-in-law by arranging their stay.

Early Marriage

Jack and Jackie's first house was at 3321 Dent Place in Georgetown, where they lived for six months. After the lease ran out, they moved to a hotel. Jackie recalled: "During the first year of our marriage we were like gypsies living in and out of a suitcase. It was turbulent. Jack made speeches all over the country and was never home more than two nights at a time."

But she found ways to adjust: "Housekeeping is a joy to me. When it all runs smoothly, when the food is good and the flowers look fresh, I have much satisfaction. I like cooking, but I'm not very good at it. I care terribly about food, but I'm not very much of a cook."

To remedy this, she signed up for cooking classes, but her first serious attempt was a little less than successful: "What a smell! I couldn't get the spoon out of the chocolate. It was like a rock. The coffee had all boiled away. I burned my arm, and it turned purple. Then Jack arrived and took me out to dinner." They also hired a full-time cook and a maid.

While they were hunting for the Georgetown house, Jackie wrote and illustrated a book for Janet: *A Book for Janet: In Case You Are Ever Thinking of Getting Married. This Is a Story to Tell You What It's Like.* One drawing was of the Capitol building late at night, with one light shining bright, and the caption "If he isn't home and that single light is on, you know the country is safe."

Before the wedding she had expressed reservations about her ability as a housekeeper to fashion designer Estelle Parker while she was being fitted for her trousseau. Parker arranged a notebook of tips for Jackie, and when she met her years later, it was still with her. "Without it I would have been lost," Jackie claimed.

One morning Jack announced that they would be having forty guests for lunch: "No one had told me anything about it. It was 11:00 A.M., and the guests were expected at one. I was in a panic. As soon as I could gather myself, I tore up to a little Greek place . . . that made wonderful casseroles.

"The luncheon was a success—casserole, salad, and raspberries. I vowed never again to be disturbed when Jack brought home unexpected guests."

Besides tending to household needs, and those of

Jack, Jackie attended an American History course at the Georgetown University School of Foreign Affairs.

Her interest in politics seems to have been new-found, as she had never cast a ballot before her marriage to Jack.

She also showed interest in Jack's career by sitting in the gallery during his important Senate speeches, reading the *Congressional Record*, and attending rallies and receptions.

After watching his Senate speeches, she would help him with his delivery, drawing on her society training and acting experience to modulate his voice and use hand gestures to make him appear more at ease and confident. She also translated passages from Voltaire and Talleyrand for him to use in his speeches.

Jackie was relieved when Jack started to indulge in Cuban cigars. "It made him less critical of my cigarette smoking."

Kennedy underwent spinal surgery in October 1954 in New York, and Jackie took responsibility for answering letters that Jack could not, including letters to Eisenhower, Lyndon Johnson (who had been elected Senate majority leader), and Vice President Richard Nixon.

She would sit with him for hours as he recovered

from his double-fusion spinal operation, feeding him, mopping his brow, playing twenty questions or checkers, reciting poems from memory, and bringing him small gifts to make him laugh. She also convinced Grace Kelly to drop in on Jack and pretend she was his new nurse. However, Jack was too tired and muddled from his medication to notice. He spent part of his recovery at Palm Beach, and before he left, his nurse taught Jackie how to dress his wound.

Jackie lived with Jean Kennedy in New York while Jack was in the hospital. During this time she discovered and started to see a new hair stylist, Kenneth Battelle at the Helena Rubenstein Beauty Salon on Fifth Avenue, and returned to him for years to come.

While Jack was convalescing at Merrywood, he followed Jackie's encouragement to write, and began to work on what would become *Profiles in Courage*. Jackie helped by taking notes on books and writing out long passages. She also found a publisher for the finished manuscript by taking it to Harper and Brothers' Cass Canfield, Lee's father-in-law.

In *Profiles*, Jack gave her acknowledgment:

This book would not have been possible without the encouragement, assistance and criticisms offered from the very beginning by my wife, Jacqueline, whose help during all the days of my convalescence, I cannot ever adequately acknowledge.

On their first trip to Europe together in July 1955, Jackie served as Jack's interpreter during meetings with Pope Pius XII and French Premier Georges Bidault, who later wrote that he had "never encountered so much wisdom invested with so much charm."

In 1962 Jackie became the first First Lady to be received by a pope. Pope John XXIII granted her the longest private audience he had ever granted—thirty-two minutes—during which they spoke mostly in French. Jackie, who had presented him with a velvet-lined vermeil letter case, said he had "centuries of kindness in his eyes."

In October 1955 the couple bought a historic property in McLean, Virginia, close to the Auchinclosses' Merrywood residence, for $125,000. Named Hickory Hill, the property included stables and a swimming pool.

Jackie redecorated the home with blue and white satin antique furniture, but paid special attention to Jack's bathroom and dressing room, arranging items so he wouldn't strain his injured back. After she became pregnant in January 1956, she focused on the nursery.

Hickory Hill was sold to Bobby and Ethel Kennedy in 1957. After delivering a stillborn child, Jackie could not bear to be in such a large house with an empty nursery.

Amid newspaper rumors that Joe Kennedy had offered Jackie one million dollars not to divorce Jack, she called and joked: "Only one million? Why not ten million?"

This rumor seems generally accepted, but makes little sense in light of the prenuptial agreement, which promised Jackie three million dollars. The document went on to explain this figure, saying that while three million seemed small compared to the Kennedy fortune, twenty million "might easily lead to the thought of an acquisition instead of a marriage."

Joe did rent the couple a house at 2808 P Street in Georgetown while they again looked for a permanent residence.

In March 1957, a few short months after Jack had decided on a run for the presidency in 1960, Jackie was again pregnant.

Starting again, they bought a house at 3307 N

Street in Georgetown. Jackie called it her "sweet little house," and remarked on how it "leans to one side, and the stairs creak."

She hired the well-known designer Sister Parish to decorate, but took an active part in decisions, made drawings, and took measurements. She had the floors painted in a white and green design, and decorated the rest of the house to match with rare tapestries and softly colored fabrics. Louis XV armchairs, Louis XVI cane dining room chairs (which later wound up in the West Sitting Room of the White House), silver lamps with chinoiserie shades, blond mahogany and Italian fruitwood tables, and copper pots for fresh flowers furnished the house.

With her inheritance from her father, she bought Jack a white Jaguar for his birthday. He almost immediately traded it in for a more practical Buick.

By 1958 she had firmly adjusted to the political life: "Politics is in my blood. I know that even if Jack changed professions, I would miss politics. It's the most exciting life imaginable—always involved with the news of the moment, meeting and working with people who are enormously alive, and every day you are caught up in something you really care about. It makes a lot of other things seem less vital. You get used to the pressure that never lets up and you learn to live with it as a fish lives in water."

Motherhood: Caroline and John

Caroline Bouvier Kennedy was born in New York City on November 27, 1957. Jackie called that day "the very happiest day of my life." She weighed seven pounds two ounces and was, in Jack's words, "as robust as a sumo wrestler."

Upset over the death of her father four months earlier, she said to Jack: "He would have been so happy, so happy. Promise me, Jack, that whether it's a boy or a girl, we will give the baby the name of Bouvier."

At three weeks Caroline was taken by Jack and Jackie to St. Patrick's Cathedral in New York and was christened by Cardinal Cushing while wearing the same robe Jackie had worn to her own christening.

They hired a British nanny, Maud Shaw, to care for Caroline. Shaw stayed with Jackie well after she moved back to New York after Jack's assassination.

After Thanksgiving dinner in 1960, Jack excused himself to fly with aides to Palm Beach. Although she was not due for another month, Jackie went into labor shortly after he left. On November 25 she gave birth to John, Jr., weighing six pounds three ounces, at Georgetown University Hospital.

The media was insatiable for news about Jackie's delivery. Once, as she was wheeled into the nursery to hold her son for the first time, a photographer sprung from a storage cabinet and attempted to snap a shot.

Jackie was highly dedicated to being the best mother her children could possibly have: "My major effort must be devoted to my children. If Caroline and John turn out badly, nothing I could do in the public eye would have any meaning," she said shortly after becoming the First Lady.

She sometimes called John, Jr., "Jack."

Maud Shaw recalled in her memoirs, "Quite often, too, we invited children we met in the park home to the Fifth Avenue apartment for dinner. Mrs. Kennedy was very good about that. I always used to ask her beforehand, of course, but her reply was always the same. 'Certainly they can come,' she would say. 'I leave it to you. I like the children to have new friends. It's good for them.' "

Jackie was careful not to be overprotective of her children, even after Jack was killed. When John was only fourteen, he went to help rebuild a Guatemalan village devastated by an earthquake. When Caroline was staying in London at age eighteen to study art at Sotheby's, a bomb went off in a car that was waiting for her. Although a bystander was killed, Jackie shelved worry that would have surely come even to a mother who hadn't seen the death of her husband and brother-in-law, and refused to call Caroline home.

On December 11, 1988, Jackie witnessed the christening of her first grandchild, Rose Schlossberg, at St. Thomas More Church in Manhattan.

Campaigns

During Jack's Senate race in 1958, Jackie addressed a crowd of eight hundred Italian-Americans in Boston's North End in fluent Italian. She was a hit, said one old-time Boston politician. "You couldn't tell the Italian-Americans of the North End that the Kennedys were Irish. No, they were Italian because Jackie spoke the language so well."

It was during the presidential primaries that Jackie first contributed to Jack's campaign strategy. Seeing his travel schedule, she thought it could be better organized and said so to Jack. "He told me to talk it over with Bob Wallace. I did and things were changed."

She would also help with speech writing by providing literary quotes and references: "I thought of some lines from a poem I thought he ought to use, and he told me to get the rest of it."

Jackie was soon making campaign speeches of her own, and her talent for foreign languages made her particularly useful: "This week I made some radio tapes appealing to Puerto Ricans, Mexican-Americans, Haitians, and Poles to register and vote. I am grateful to my parents for the effort they made to teach us foreign languages. All these people have contributed so much to our country's culture, it seems a proper courtesy to address them in their own tongue."

Wisconsin was particularly important to Jack, but he had to be in Washington during the primary to vote on important civil rights legislation. "You go back to Washington and vote, Jack," she said. "I'll carry on for you." She did just that, moving quickly through towns and giving speeches to large and small crowds.

At one stop in Kenosha, Wisconsin, she charmed the manager of a supermarket into letting her use the store's public address system. "Just keep on with your shopping while I tell you about my husband, John F. Kennedy," she announced before going on to detail his political and military career. She concluded with "Please vote for him."

Jack carried the state by 106,000 votes.

But pregnant with John, Jr., Jackie couldn't stay on the campaign trail for long. Back in Georgetown, she contributed by writing a syndicated national column called *Campaign Wife*, discussing education, what she would do as First Lady ("I wouldn't put on a mask and pretend to be something I wasn't"), and health care.

To a friend who remarked that it would be good politics to deliver John, Jr., on the day before votes were cast, she replied: "Oh, I hope not. I'd have to get up and vote the next day."

To reporters after the election, she described herself as "the woman who has everything, including the next president of the United States."

She also at this time thought it important to write her autobiography. Close friend Mary Van Rensselaer offered to work with Jackie on the project, which was serialized in *Ladies' Home Journal*, which paid $150,000 for four installments. The biography was then expanded and published by Doubleday, the company Jackie would join as editor in 1977, as *Jacqueline Bouvier Kennedy*, by Mary Van Rensselaer in 1961.

— CAMPAIGNING WITH JOHN FITZGERALD KENNEDY IN NEW YORK —

IV

The First Lady

Adjustments

During her recovery from John's birth, she received a letter from Eleanor Roosevelt, offering friendly advice on being First Lady "Most things are made easier, though I think on the whole, life is rather difficult for both the children and their parents in the 'fishbowl' that lies before you."

Jackie spoke to reporters about changes she would have to make as First Lady in 1960:

Reporter: "When you are First Lady, you won't be able to jump into your car and rush down to Orange County to go fox hunting."

Jackie: "You couldn't be more wrong. That is one thing I won't give up."

Reporter: "But you'll have to make some concessions to the role, won't you?"

Jackie: "Oh, I will. I'll wear hats."

Jackie described her conception of what her duties would be in the White House on the *Today* show, September 15, 1960:

> I have always thought the main duty is to preserve the President of the United States so he can be of best service to his country, and that means running a household smoothly around him, and helping him in any way he might ask you to.

Jackie's own favorite First Lady was Bess Truman, wife of Harry S Truman, from Missouri, who was known for her serious, no-frills approach to running the Truman household. Jackie's comment on her was, "She brought a daughter to the White House at a most difficult age and managed to keep her from being spoiled so that she has made a happy marriage with lovely children of her own. Mrs. Truman kept her family close together in spite of White House demands, and that is the hardest thing to do."

On the day John, Jr., was baptized at the chapel at Georgetown University Hospital, Jackie took her first look at the White House on a tour conducted by Mamie Eisenhower. Still exhausted and feeling faint, under doctor's orders she requested to be taken through the rooms in a wheelchair. Her situation was serious: she had been warned at the hospital that if she attempted to climb stairs, she could die. However, when she arrived for the tour, no wheelchair was provided. Rather than complain, she stoically walked through the tour, but then became seriously ill almost immediately upon her return to Georgetown.

In December, when she and John, Jr., were recuperating in Palm Beach, she left the Kennedy compound with Jack for church. Waiting outside the compound was Richard Pavlick, who believed that Jack had bought the election and planned to kill him by ramming his car into the Kennedys' while simultaneously lighting the seven sticks of dynamite he carried. But when he saw Jackie, he paused. "I did not wish to harm her or the children. I decided to get him at the church or later," he explained to the Secret Service. Jackie, terribly shaken, was reported to have said: "We're nothing but sitting ducks in a shooting gallery."

Shortly after the inauguration, Jackie told her secretary that she didn't want the typical title applied to her: "The one thing I do not want to be called is First Lady. It sounds like a saddle horse. Would you notify the telephone operators and everyone else that I'm to be known simply as Mrs. Kennedy and not as First Lady."

To the Secret Service she was known by her code name, "Lace."

After the inauguration, she expressed concern about the public spotlight: "I felt as though I had just turned into a piece of property. It's frightening to lose your anonymity at thirty-one."

Gallup polls found that from 1960 to 1966, Jackie was considered the most admired woman in the world.

History in the Making

Jackie frequently redecorated the White House Treaty Room for important signings. For the signing of the Nuclear Test Ban Treaty in 1963, she replaced the standard Victorian desk with their Louis XVI desk, not only to make more room for dignitaries, but so that the signing would take place on a family heirloom. She even had the commemorative plaque of the signing fixed to the desk.

Jackie first met André Malraux, French minister of culture, on her trip to Paris in 1961. After visiting the Kennedys the following year, and being again charmed by Jackie, he cleared the way for the *Mona Lisa* to visit America for the first time. Rather than lend the piece directly to a museum, he made the loan to President Kennedy, who in turn arranged for it to be shown at the National Gallery of Art.

White House Renovation

After her first tour of the White House, Jackie was disappointed with the nation's most famous address, to say the least:

> Oh, God. It's the worst place in the world. So cold and dreary. A dungeon like the Lubyanka. It looks like it's been furnished by discount stores. I've never seen anything like it. I can't bear the thought of moving in. I hate it, hate it, hate it.

Jackie further disparaged the White House's decor as "early Statler," and commented on the overuse of "Mamie Eisenhower pink," to her the height of bad taste, and set about redecorating. She had the upstairs family quarters done by American designer Sister Parish in an inviting, comfortable style, while the main floor State Rooms were done by Stephanie Boudin, master of the Paris decorating firm House of Jansen, which had restored the palace of Versailles and held clients such as the Duke and Duchess of Windsor.

"Everything in the White House must have a reason for being there," said Jackie. "It would be a sacrilege merely to redecorate—a word I hate. It must be restored. And that has nothing to do with decoration. That is a question of scholarship."

Jackie had made use of her recovery from John's birth to study the history of the White House and its decor, and greatly impressed the White House curators and groundskeepers with her knowledge. "When she arrived at 1600 Pennsylvania Avenue she knew as much about it as any historian possibly could," said James Roe Ketchum, curator of the White House during the Kennedy administration.

One of her first moves was to persuade Congress to designate the White House a National Museum, which opened funding avenues and guaranteed that her work would be preserved.

Using her charm and connections in the world of art collectors, Jackie secured over 160 donated paintings for the White House walls. One of these was from Philadelphia publisher Walter Annenberg, who owned a portrait of Benjamin Franklin. Jackie wrote to him: "You, Mr. Annenberg, are the first citizen of Philadelphia. And in his day, Benjamin Franklin was the first citizen of Philadelphia. And that's why, Mr. Annenberg, I thought of you. Do you think a great Philadelphia citizen would give the White House a portrait of another great Philadelphia citizen?" He did donate the painting, which had cost him $250,000.

After finding the rug she wanted for the private dining room, she balked when she heard the price — $10,000. She wrote a memo to the chief usher. "I so like the rug but we are short of dollars and I am ENRAGED at everyone trying to gyp the White House. Tell him if he gives it he can get a tax donation and photo in our book — if not — goodbye!" The dealer agreed to donate the rug.

The restoration went into incredible detail: $12,500 was spent on carefully removing antique wallpaper from a historic Maryland house and putting it up in the Diplomatic Room. The overhead lights in the dining room, which Jackie felt deepened the lines in women's faces, were replaced with sconces whose candles gave off a kinder, diffused light.

Mirrors were removed ("If there's anything I can't stand, it's Victorian mirrors—off to the dungeons with them"), walls were repainted, and shades were replaced ("They are enormous and they have pulleys and ropes. After pulling them down, I feel like a sailor taking in a sail.").

Jackie also thoroughly explored the White House basement and storage facilities. Her treasure hunts uncovered Lincoln's china, a Bellange pier table, and Monroe's gold and silver flatware.

One area that was off-limits to her restoration was the White House bomb shelter. After demanding to see it, and being informed that it was also a command post for Signal Corps, she said:

How amazing! I didn't expect to find so much humanity! I thought it would be a great big room that we could use as an indoor recreation room for the children. I even had plans for a basketball court in there!

Sister Parish added a kitchen, pantry, and dining room to the private family unit on the second floor, where the bedroom of Mamie Eisenhower's mother was. This allowed the First Family to cook and snack without having to go downstairs to the State Dining Room to be served.

Maintenance of the White House was just as important. Jackie issued a housekeeping memo in 1961 that detailed the daily cleanup:

All 18 bedrooms and 20 baths on the second floor must be tidied; 147 windows kept clean; 29 fireplaces laid ready for lighting; 412 doorknobs polished; 3,000 square feet of floorspace on 2nd story waxed and buffed; half an acre of marble mopped and remopped; carpeting vacuumed three times a day; 37 rooms on ground floor dusted twice daily.

Jackie gave the project of restoring the spot of lawn outside Kennedy's office, which would become known as the White House Rose Garden to her friend Bunny Mellon, an expert horticulturist. The Rose Garden is now well known as a site for important press gatherings and signings. Jackie said of the garden: "The beauty of it seems to affect even hard-bitten reporters who come there just to watch what is going on."

Jackie put all she had learned into *The White House:*

An Historic Guide, which was published by the National Geographic Society in July 1962. The first printing of 250,000 copies was sold out within three months, and the book was taken back to press in the fall and winter of 1962. To date, over 4,400,000 copies have been sold, making it one of the best-selling guidebooks of all time. Proceeds from the book have greatly helped the White House restoration fund Jackie established in November 1961.

The first issue of *Newsweek* in 1962 praised Jackie's accomplishments: "Jacqueline Kennedy has made more changes in the White House than any woman in its 143 years. This alone entitles her to at least a footnote in history. Her style and influence could easily give her some highly readable paragraphs in the main text of history."

When she thought she had brought the White House decor up to an acceptable standard, she took a CBS reporter on a guided tour in 1962, which was watched by over forty-six million viewers and won Emmy and Peabody awards. Jackie wrote the script herself, and spoke without notes or TelePrompTers. She told viewers that her favorite president was Lincoln, but she felt the strongest affinity toward Jefferson.

Social and State Functions

Frank Sinatra and Peter Lawford threw the first official event for the president and First Lady on the eve of the inauguration, January 19, 1961, at the National Guard Armory on the east side of Washington. Before the gala, Jackie and Jack dined with the Grahams, owners of the *Washington Post*, and attended a concert at Constitution Hall.

As they drove from one event to the next, crowds gathered along the routes. Jack asked that the lights in the limousine be turned on so the public could see Jackie.

Performers at the gala, who took no pay for their appearances, included Mahalia Jackson, Frank Sinatra, Ella Fitzgerald, Gene Kelly, Laurence Olivier, Ethel Merman, Jimmy Durante, Harry Belafonte, Bette Davis, Janet Leigh, and Tony Curtis.

Saying that at White House parties the marine band sat between numbers like "mournful bellhops," Jackie insisted that they play continually through events.

Jackie's preferred seating arrangements for state dinners was ten at a table, always round, to allow her guests to feel more relaxed and conversant. The tables were decorated with fresh, modest flowers such as anemones, freesia, bachelor's buttons, tulips, or lily of the valley. Her tableware was old vermeil and she bought her crystal in Morgantown, West Virginia, where Jack had won an extraordinary victory in the primaries.

She also had something to say about introductions. "Will you tell whoever it is, after this—at *every* occasion when they play 'Hail to the Chief' and just announce the president—to please also say the vice president of the United States and Mrs. Johnson. It is so embarrassing to have them not announced and then just disappear like maids."

Jackie hired her childhood schoolmate from Chapin, Nancy Tuckerman, as social secretary after Letitia Baldridge left the White House. Recalls Tuckerman: "When I came to the White House in April 1963, Jackie wanted the first state dinner to be memorable, to set the tone."

The guest of honor was the king of Afghanistan, and Jackie agreed to a fireworks display on the South Lawn. Jack asked that the time allotted to the display be cut in half, but the producer used the same amount of fireworks in half the time. "There was an explosion you wouldn't believe. The king's bodyguards and Secret Service men jumped into place. The White House switchboard was inundated. It was thought a plane had crashed into the White House," said Tuckerman.

On their first trip to Europe together as First Family, Jack and Jackie were greeted in France with a 101-gun salute and crowds of admirers screaming, "Jacqui!"

Uncomfortable with the gifts foreign heads of state would lavish on Jackie, Jack sent an aide to ask her to send them back. Jack was particularly concerned about the horses given to her by the king of Saudi Arabia, the president of Pakistan, and the prime minister of Ireland. She responded to the aide: "I understand what you're saying, but there's a problem. I want the horses."

One gift she perhaps wasn't as attached to, but had in fact asked for, was Pushinka, a puppy of one of the dogs the Soviets had sent into space, presented by Soviet Ambassador Menshikov. "I'm afraid I asked Mr. Khrushchev for it in Vienna. I was just running out of things to say."

She was taken with Mrs. Khrushchev: "I liked her. She was the kind of woman you'd ask in perfect confidence to baby-sit for you, if you wanted to go out some evening."

At a White House dinner, Jack displayed his pride

in his wife's linguistic ability. Leaning over to the wife of the French ambassador, he said, "Jackie speaks fluent French. But I only understand one out of every five words she says—and that word is de Gaulle." De Gaulle himself commented to Jack, "Your wife knows more French history than any Frenchwoman."

Her skills and the love the French had for Jackie were not unnoticed by President Johnson in the years to come. According to Kennedy White House Press Secretary Pierre Salinger, Johnson wanted to nominate her ambassador to France, but she dissuaded him.

Determined to create a center of the arts and scholarship at the White House, Jackie made figures such as Robert Frost, Isaiah Berlin, and Leonard Bernstein presidential guests. She built a stage in the East Room, which hosted performances from Pablo Casals, Igor Stravinsky, George Balanchine, and the Metropolitan Opera Studio, which presented portions of Mozart's "Cosi Van Tutti." Composers who answered her invitations included Aaron Copland, Samuel Barber, Elliot Carter, Virgil Thomson, William Schuman, and Douglas Moore.

Jackie gave her husband the idea to have a special White House dinner for the 1962 Nobel Laureates on

April 29, 1962; 175 guests attended in addition to the 49 Laureates.

Her efforts earned her the title "unofficial minister of culture," in the *New York Times*.

After her return from her first trip to Paris as First Lady, she insisted that fine French wine and champagne be featured at all White House functions. Her preference was for Dom Perignon, but there was always one token bottle of American wine at the table.

Jack often turned to Jackie for insights into the minds of foreign leaders. Senator George Smathers said, "She went to India, Pakistan, Greece, Italy, and other places, and people thought she was merely vacationing. But she was doing far more than that. She was spending time with government officials, buttering them up. She was taking mental notes."

Jackie was again invaluable on a visit to Miami to see the veterans of the Bay of Pigs invasion, where she delivered a rousing speech in Spanish, and was sent to New York to see UN Ambassador Adlai Stevenson, with whom Jack had a strained relationship.

Escape

Jackie found a friend in Joan Kennedy, Teddy's wife. The two were the youngest of the Kennedy women, and found they both had a need to get away from the demands of being a politician's wife. Jackie said once to Joan: "They have no idea what we do when we're alone. I know you go over to Squaw Island by yourself and play the piano, and I go off alone and paint, and they think we're weird because we're alone. They can't stand to be alone."

But aside from being alone, they also enjoyed being together. Joan tells of how they used to get away: "We would get a Secret Service man to drive her speedboat and go waterskiing. Jackie would go first and then she would rest and I would go, and that was enough for me, but she was very very good, and she would go again. Then the two of us were dropped off a mile away from the harbor and we swam back in together. We did this the whole time she was First Lady, and nobody knew about it."

Jackie herself designed a one-story house for herself and John F. Kennedy in the early White House years. The house, known as Wexford, was contractor-built on Rattlesnake Mountain in Atoka, Virginia. She and the president occupied the house only four times before his death.

Jackie made thirteen trips abroad as First Lady. However, she never accompanied Jack on his domestic presidential visits. Her fateful trip to Dallas was an exception. She told friends: "It's a tiny sacrifice on my part for something he feels is very important to him."

By January 1963, Jackie was feeling overextended and ready to recommit herself to motherhood: "I'm taking the veil. I've had it with being First Lady all the time, and now I'm going to give more attention to my children. I want you to cut off *all* outside activity — whether it's a glass of sherry with a poet or coffee with a king. No more art gallery dedications — no nothing — unless absolutely necessary."

— J.F.K.'s Funeral with Bobby and Ted —

V.

Tragedy and Recovery

Lost Children

Jackie suffered from a history of problems relating to pregnancy, a problem doctors attributed to stress. Her first pregnancy ended in a miscarriage in the third month of October 1955, just days after moving into their new Hickory Hill home.

She became pregnant again in January 1956, but after a long season of politicking, including an appearance at the Democratic National Convention, she miscarried again on August 23, 1956. She had been rushed to the hospital, and an attempt was made to save the baby by cesarean section. The stillborn girl remained unnamed. The cause was listed as "exhaustion and nervous tension following the Democratic National Convention."

Jack was sailing at the time, off the coast of Italy,

but his brother Bobby consoled Jackie and even arranged for the child's burial.

Despite Jack's absence, she said of him during her recovery: "He is a rock, and I lean on him for everything. He is so kind. Ask anyone who works for him! And he's never irritable or sulky. He would do anything I wanted or give me anything I wanted."

Jackie announced to the world on April 18, 1963, that she and Jack were expecting their third child. On August 7, 1963, Jackie felt the first labor pains. Although she had planned to deliver at Walter Reed Army Hospital in Washington, an emergency contingency plan was put into action: Jackie was flown by helicopter from Squaw Island to a ten-room suite at Otis Air Force Base's hospital. By cesarean, she delivered four-pound one-ounce Patrick Bouvier Kennedy. He was baptized immediately and flown to Children's Hospital in Boston. He died there three days later. Jackie was sedated and remained too ill to attend either the funeral in Cardinal Cushing's private chapel or the burial at the Kennedy family plot at Holyrood Cemetery, Brookline.

While pregnant, Jackie had prepared a White House nursery for Patrick, complete with white crib, curtains, and rug contrasting with the blue walls.

The Assassination

Jackie said that when she first heard the shots, she thought it was a motorcycle backfiring.

Her widely reported reaction was: "My God, what are they doing? My God, they've killed Jack, they've killed my husband."

The six seconds that left a president dead have been interpreted in dozens of ways. Jackie was accused of trying to flee out of the back of the car, of not covering her husband to protect him from the second shot, of having panicked and abandoned him to save herself. Other views hold her actions as futile heroism—reaching over the trunk of the car to save a section of his skull, or to help a Secret Service agent into the accelerating vehicle.

Jackie refused to leave Jack's side when they arrived at Parkland Memorial Hospital. Dr. George Buckley, JFK's personal physician, offered her a sedative, which she refused. "I don't want a sedative, I want to be with my husband when he dies."

In the trauma room, she dropped on one knee to pray. When she arose, she was told Jack was dead. "I know," she said.

The president and First Lady had been given red roses at Love Field, which became scattered across the

81

backseat of the car. A doctor at Parkland Memorial Hospital solemnly gave her two red roses found under Kennedy's shirt. Before leaving, she gave one back to him.

Before joining Jack in the hearse to take them to the airport, Jackie slipped her wedding ring on his finger.

When given an opportunity to change from her bloodied clothes for the flight back to Washington and the swearing in of President Johnson, she replied: "No, let them see what they have done."

Jackie requested that her children be kept from hearing the news of Jack's death until she could tell them personally, thirty-six hours after it had occurred.

She wrote to Richard M. Nixon shortly after the assassination. "I knew his death could have been prevented, and I will never cease to torture myself with that. . . . Whoever thought such a hideous thing could happen in this country? I know how you must feel, so closely missing the greatest prize . . . and now you must commit all your family's hopes and efforts again. Just one thing I would say to you. If it does not work out as you have hoped for so long, please be consoled by what you have—your life and your family. We never value life enough."

Jackie was only thirty-four when her husband was killed.

In 1968 she quietly objected to Robert F. Kennedy running for president. "They will do to him what they did to Jack," she told Arthur Schlesinger in March 1968. In June Bobby Kennedy was killed by an assassin after winning the California primary.

The Funeral

While his family was of the opinion that Jack should be buried near Boston, Jackie felt the best way to honor him was at Arlington National Cemetery; Jack now belonged to the people and to history.

She visited Arlington for the first time the day after he was killed, and after standing on a green slope with views of the Lincoln Memorial and Washington Monument across the Potomac, she chose the spot. Jack had visited Arlington several months before, and had commented on one spot just below the Curtis-Lee Mansion, on how the view was so marvelous he could have stayed there forever. Jackie was evidently looking for this very spot.

Only military veterans, their spouses, and their unmarried children may be buried at Arlington.

After the assassination, Jackie directed that the funeral ceremony should follow that of Abraham Lincoln, and that Jack's coffin would be drawn by the same caisson that had carried the coffin of Franklin D. Roosevelt. She picked a horse, oddly enough named Black Jack, to follow the coffin without a rider in its saddle, and with boots turned backward in the stirrups. Subdued drumrolls would mark the progress of the procession from the sidelines.

She insisted on official treatment of Jack. "I don't want any undertakers. I want everything done by the navy."

As his body lay in state in the East Room of the White House, an honor guard composed of one member of each of the armed forces stood by. Breaking with tradition, Jackie insisted that the guards look at the coffin, instead of away from it.

She told Caroline to write letters to their father, "and tell him how much you love him." John, Jr., at three years old still too young to write, scribbled on Caroline's letter. The letters were placed in Jack's coffin, along with her wedding band, which was returned to her after the autopsy, a letter Jackie had herself written to Jack the night before, samples of scrimshaw, a bracelet Jack had given her, and gold cuff links that she had given him.

84

After carefully arranging the items around Jack, she clipped a lock of his hair.

Jackie had architect John Warnecke commissioned for the memorial at Arlington.

The funeral took place on November 25, 1963, which was also John, Jr.'s, third birthday. They had a small birthday party for him that evening—his gifts included a copy of *Peter Rabbit* and a toy helicopter. Jackie and Bobby Kennedy visited Jack's grave site at midnight, and prayed next to the eternal flame.

She gave gentle instructions to her children throughout the service. As the navy band played "Hail to the Chief," Jackie told John, Jr., "John, you can salute your daddy now and say good-bye to him." And to Caroline, after the eulogies, "We're going to say good-bye to Daddy, and we're going to kiss him good-bye and tell Daddy how much we love him and how much we'll always miss him." As they leaned over to kiss the flag draped over his coffin, Caroline put her hand under the flag, as if to be closer.

It was her choice to walk the half mile from the funeral service to Arlington Cemetery, refusing, she said, to ride "in a fat, black Cadillac." Following her lead, foreign heads of state and associates, including

85

Presidents Johnson and de Gaulle, chose to walk the route as well.

A British journalist wrote for his paper: "Jacqueline Kennedy has today given her country the one thing it has always lacked, and that is majesty."

Building a New Life

Jackie wrote to President Johnson the day after the funeral. "But more than that we were friends, all four of us. All you did for me as a friend and the happy times we had. I always thought, way before the nomination, that Lady Bird should be the First Lady — but I don't need to tell you here what I think of her qualities — her extraordinary grace of character — her willingness to assume every burden."

She also commented on her preparations to leave the White House: "It was so strange last night. I was wandering through this house."

She closed the letter with: "It cannot be very much help to you your first day in office to hear children on the lawn at recess. It is just one more example of your kindness that you let them stay — I promise they will soon be gone."

Jackie stayed in the White House for eleven days after the assassination.

She had a plaque mounted in their bedroom, which read "In this room lived John Fitzgerald Kennedy with his wife Jacqueline during the two years, ten months, and two days he was President of the United States — January 20, 1961–November 22, 1963." The only other commemorative plaque in the room was to Abraham Lincoln, but the Kennedy plaque was removed by First Lady Pat Nixon.

She also wrote to Khrushchev on December 1, 1963: "You and [Jack] were adversaries, but you were allied in a determination that the world should not be blown up. You respected each other and could deal with each other. I know that President Johnson will make every effort to establish the same relationship with you."

After leaving the White House, Jackie and her children moved to a house in Georgetown lent to her by a sympathetic couple at 3038 N Street. By mid-December, Jackie bought a house across the street, at 3017 N Street, for $195,000. At this house Jackie got a taste of things to come: the sidewalk was crowded with tourists and curiosity-seekers. The Secret Service and Metro Police had to clear a path through the crowd. Women would often break the police lines to attempt to hug her children. Tour buses made stops on her street.

She had just finished redecorating in fall 1964 when she decided to move to New York, worried about the crowd's effect on her children and the memories Washington evoked. The family first moved to a suite at the Hotel Carlyle on Madison Avenue, until they found the fifteen-room apartment at 1040 Fifth Avenue where Jackie lived until her death in 1994.

She paid only $200,000 for the apartment in 1964, but it was worth close to $4 million when she died.

Jean Kennedy Smith and Stephen Smith lived only a block away, as did her sister Lee and her husband, Stanislas Radziwill.

She received the usual amount from the government granted to widows of presidents: $10,000 a year for life or until remarriage, and free mailing privileges.

From the John F. Kennedy estate, she received only $70,000 cash, an annual allowance of $200,000 from a trust fund, his home at the Kennedy compound, and most of his personal effects.

Besides her children, one focus of the first year of her life was the founding of the John F. Kennedy Memorial Library. She raised over $10 million with one single televised appeal and received an annual allocation of $50,000 from Congress for staff and postage.

On the first anniversary of the assassination,

Jackie wrote a brief piece for *Look* magazine: "What was lost cannot be replaced. I should have known that it was asking too much to dream that I might have grown old with him. . . ."

Perhaps her first social event after the assassination was a "teeny, tiny" party given by her sister at her apartment for "less than a hundred," in Lee's pleading words. The party was also attended by Leonard Bernstein, Pierre Salinger, and Bobby and Ethel. Jackie stayed until four in the morning.

Jackie continued to receive Secret Service protection after Jack's assassination. Regulations at the time of Jack's assassination were that widows of presidents would receive protection for two years. This was increased to four, and then in 1968, when Jackie's protection would have expired, it was extended to death or remarriage.

Jackie began meditating and practicing yoga in 1967 as a way of coping with her life's tragedies. She told Marlon Brando that she had learned meditation and a few yoga positions, including one that had her standing on her head, from Indian Prime Minister Nehru during her visit to India.

Jackie is supposed to have carried on an affair with JFK's deputy defense secretary and friend, Roswell Gilpatric, after she recovered from the assassination. The affair ended shortly before her engagement to Onassis. It would have probably remained secret if letters from Jackie to Gilpatric had not been stolen from his law office by a lawyer from the firm who was discovered to be the thief when he attempted to have the letters auctioned in 1970. Mr. Gilpatric died in March 1996.

The press also speculated on a romance with British diplomat Sr. William David Ormsby-Gore, who had served as ambassador to the United States for part of the Kennedy administration. A cousin of his had married Kathleen Kennedy, Jack's younger sister, in 1944, but he had been killed in World War II, while she died in a plane crash in 1948. Another Kennedy connection was that he had known Jack's father, Joseph, when he was ambassador to England in the late 1930s. Due to these connections and the fact that in 1967 Jackie had accompanied Ormsby-Gore on trips to Ireland, Cambodia, and Thailand, the press saw engagement as a certain fact, and were likely disappointed when none materialized.

— Jackie at Her Wedding to Aristotle Onassis, 1968, Skorpios Island, Greece —

VI

Years of Privacy

Avoiding the Public Eye

After her husband's assassination, Jackie gave a final interview to Theodore White, a journalist she trusted highly, for *Life* magazine on November 29, 1963. Afterward she gave only a handful of interviews and only under strict conditions.

In her *Life* interview with Theodore White, she gave the public a word to remember the Kennedy administration by: "The lines he loved to hear were: 'Don't let it be forgot, that once there was a spot, for one brief shining moment that was known as Camelot.'"

She controlled the conditions of the interview tightly, reading over the typescript and making corrections. The magazine held the presses that night, running up an extra $30,000 in overtime, waiting for

White to read the story to editors from a phone in the White House kitchen at two in the morning, with Jackie standing close by.

White wrote in his memoirs about the conditions for the interview, saying that Jackie wanted him to "rescue Jack from all those 'bitter people' who were going to write about him in history."

Jackie gave another interview, to William Manchester for his work on a definitive book on the assassination. Although he had secured permission from the Kennedys and Jackie, and agreed with his publisher that his royalties and most of the profits would be handed over to the JFK Library, he also arranged to have the book serialized in *Look*, for which he would be paid $665,000. This development caused Jackie to seek an injunction against publication. The case was settled in 1967, and the interview, which runs 313 minutes and contains intimate details about her family life, was sealed at her request, and will remain so at the John F. Kennedy Memorial Library until 2067.

Jackie granted an interview to publishing trade journal *Publishers Weekly* in 1993, and only under the conditions that it would not stray from discussion of her work as a book editor, that no photographs would be taken, and no tape recording made.

She was also granted her often-refused request of editorial approval over the article. However, she made only one minor grammatical correction to the manuscript.

On May 25, 1972, Jackie agreed to an interview with Maryam Kharazmi, reporter for the English-language newspaper *Kayham International.* In this interview she explained her aversion to the press:

> The truth of the matter is that I am a very shy person. People take my diffidence for arrogance and my withdrawal from publicity as a sign, supposedly, that I am looking down on the rest of mankind. I get afraid of reporters when they come to me in a crowd. I don't like crowds because I don't like impersonal masses. They remind me of swarms of locusts.

Her views of the press had arisen long before her private years. While in the White House, reporters cornered her with a new German shepherd puppy, and asked her what she planned to feed it. "Reporters," she replied.

After her husband's assassination, she never posed for a formal press photograph.

In the early 1970s she took legal action against

photographer Ronald Galella to prevent him from approaching her or her children. She charged that he was harassing her and invading her privacy, and he immediately countersued, saying that through her suit, she was interfering with his livelihood. Aristotle Onassis asked for a settlement, but Galella demanded $100,000. Jackie's suit prevailed, and he was prohibited from coming within fifty yards of Jackie and her children.

Only once were photographers allowed into Jackie's meticulously designed New York apartment: in 1971 she authorized two photos, of her library and dining room, to run in *House Beautiful* in order to help promote the fabrics of Design Works of Bedford-Stuyvesant, a black-owned enterprise in Brooklyn.

In the early 1980s Jackie commissioned architect Hugh Newell Jacobsen to design her vacation home on the 365 acres of land on Martha's Vineyard she had bought in 1978 for around $1,100,000. The architect was sworn to secrecy about the commission, which turned out to be a $4.5 million, 3,100-square-foot hideaway with ten rooms, a 900-square-foot guesthouse, stable, and a silo which she had transformed into a space for John, Jr.

Jackie became entangled in a land dispute with a

group of Wampanoag Indians soon after she bought the property. The issue was resolved ten years later with a complicated land swap.

The main attraction Martha's Vineyard held for her was privacy. Although she ventured out to local shops and restaurants, her house was remote and accessible only by boat or a single, well-guarded road. Said *People* magazine of her site: "Ironically, Jackie's choice of location may insure her more privacy that even money can buy. Some islanders cherish Gay Head's seclusion even more than she — they cultivate marijuana in its dark woods."

She could be seen often in Martha's Vineyard, cycling, waterskiing, and taking her motorboat, with registration number MS PT109, out on Menemsha Pond.

She also kept a home in Bernardsville, New Jersey, where she could easily get away to ride horses. She had bought the estate and ten surrounding acres in 1974 for $200,000 and sold it to her children in 1992 for $100.

In New York, after Aristotle's death, Jackie constantly made attempts to live normally. She did her own shopping at Lobel's Prime Meats on Madison Avenue and Eighty-third, stopped in at lunch counters near work for burgers, and shopped at the Gap on Eighty-sixth and Madison for jeans and sweatpants.

She enjoyed films at the Trans-Lux on Madison Avenue, close to her home. To avoid unwanted attention, she would send a maid to buy tickets beforehand, arrive after the lights had dimmed, and leave as soon as the movie ended.

She was committed to exercise, working out several times a week at the Vertical Club on Sixtieth Street, a gym frequented by celebrities.

Throughout her life, Jackie maintained a weight of between 123 and 133 pounds.

Social Circles

By 1966 Jackie appeared to have shaken off the grief of Jack's death, and was spotted in various social scenes in New York. Jackie preferred the company of writers and composers to that of elder statesmen ("I'm still too young for all that," she said), and was seen with Leonard Bernstein, Truman Capote, Irwin Shaw, Stephen Sondheim, Mike Nichols, Marlon Brando, and Frank Sinatra. In 1966 she toured the Seville Fair on horseback wearing a crimson jacket and a broad-brimmed hat and drinking sherry.

For the January 13, 1975, issue of *The New Yorker*,

Jackie contributed an anonymous piece to the "Talk of the Town" department, called "Being Present," which describes her being transfixed by the Manhattan sunlight. "Accompanied by Mr. Katz, we left the Metropolitan and walked up the Park side of Fifth Avenue in bright sunlight. We stopped at the corner of Ninety-fourth Street and looked across at the facade of what is still known as Audubon House, a six-story Georgian building of red brick, with shiny black shutters. Lovely it is."

In the seventies and eighties, Jackie entertained frequently at her Fifth Avenue apartment. Henry Kissinger, Robert S. McNamara, Arthur Schlesinger, Jr., John Kenneth Galbraith, Candice Bergen, George Plimpton, Roger Mudd, Barbara Walters, and Rudolph Nureyev were all frequent guests.

In the seventies she became friendly with Gloria Steinem, who is widely credited with giving her the inspiration to seek out a career. Steinem encouraged her to later write an article for *Ms.*, explaining why she chose to work. The article, running fourteen hundred words, was published in March 1979.

After the death of Aristotle, she was seen on what could be dates with George McGovern, Tiffany & Company President Henry Platt, Pete Hamill, and

Frank Sinatra. She was also escorted by William Walton, journalist and artist and former coordinator for JFK's presidential campaign; Senator Charles Mathias, Jr.; and Michael Cacoyannis, director of *Zorba the Greek*.

With Maurice Templesman, she was seen frequently in the company of Walter Cronkite, Billy Joel, Beverly Sills, Carly Simon, Katherine Graham, Jules Feiffer, Mike Wallace, Spike Lee, Robert McNamara, and Vernon Jordan at restaurants on Martha's Vineyard.

Aristotle Socrates Onassis

Onassis was raised in the city of Smyrna, but fled to Buenos Aires with his sister when the Ottoman Turks invaded the city in 1923. He was only sixteen and left with a mere $60 in his pocket.

His shipping company employed three thousand and his fleet was one of the largest in the world, surpassing even the navies of many countries.

His first marriage was in 1946 at age thirty-nine, to Tina Livanos, the seventeen-year-old daughter of another shipping magnate. His son, Alexander, was born in 1948, and his daughter, Christina, in 1950. Tina sued for divorce in 1960, charging adultery.

100

In 1954 Onassis had been arrested and indicted in the United States on charges of illegally acquiring surplus ships from the United States government through dummy corporations. The criminal charges were dropped after being tied up in court for two years, and Onassis paid $7 million to settle civil charges.

While she was recovering from the loss of Patrick, Jackie's sister Lee arranged for her to pay a visit to Aristotle's 325-foot yacht, *Christina*, for a cruise of the Greek islands in 1963.

Jack was concerned about appearances, and so he sent Franklin Roosevelt, Jr., then undersecretary of commerce, and his wife as chaperones. He might not have worried, however. Aristotle did not appear on his own ship until late in the cruise, although he had hired extra crewmen and a dance band to make Jackie's stay enjoyable.

At the end of the cruise, Aristotle presented Jackie with a diamond and ruby necklace. This would be only the opening salvo in an onslaught of jewelry that he would lavish her with throughout their marriage. For her fortieth birthday he gave her a diamond necklace and bracelet worth over a million dollars. Aristotle was one of the guests invited to Jack's funeral who stayed at the White House after the services. After she moved to New York, Ari took her to dinner, where she talked about Jack and cried several times. For several years afterward, he would frequently stay at the Kennedy compound in Hyannis, but rumors of romance never appeared.

Over the next three years, Aristotle occasionally called and took Jackie to ballets, concerts, and dinners. In 1968 he proposed to her on his yacht, but she did not give an immediate answer.

To clear the way for his upcoming marriage to Jackie, Ari broke off his ten-year relationship with opera singer Maria Callas. Callas complained that Onassis was only furthering his collection of famous, beautiful women.

Criticism of Jackie for her engagement to Aristotle came from around the world. A Swedish newspaper ran "Jackie, How Could You" as a headline. Closer to home, the reports were more caustic: "Why Did Jackie Marry Onassis? There Are Well Over a Billion Reasons," read the headline of the *Long Island Press*.

Jackie did have Aristotle agree to a three-million-dollar cash payment upon marriage; however, her view of the marriage was more innocent: "You don't know how lonely I've been," she said to a friend.

Jackie and Ari were married on October 10, 1968,

on Onassis' private island of Skorpios in the Ionian Sea. Jackie wore a $1.2 million ring topped with a huge heart-shaped ruby surrounded by diamonds where she once wore Jack's plain wedding band.

The simple ceremony was attended by only twenty-one guests, who gathered in Skorpios' Chapel of the Little Mother of God. On Jackie's side of the aisle were Caroline and John; Janet and Hugh Auchincloss; Pat Lawford and Jean Smith; Prince and Princess Stanislas Radziwill and their two children. On the bridegroom's side, his two children; Mrs. Aremis Garofalides; Ari's sister, half sister, her husband, his niece, and her husband; Mr. and Mrs. Nicholas Kokims, who were friends and business partners; and John Georgakis, managing director of Olympic Airways, and his wife.

The ceremony was Greek Orthodox. Rose Kennedy refused to attend.

Both of Aristotle's children objected strongly to the match.

Also disapproving, the Vatican deemed that Jackie would be living in mortal sin with Ari because of his previous marriage and his Greek Orthodox heritage. Cardinal Cushing, who officiated at Jack and Jackie's wedding, refused to condemn the match, and resigned two years before he was due to retire. "Why can't she marry whoever she wants to?" he asked.

She was ultimately barred from receiving sacraments from the Catholic Church, but was not excommunicated. The door was left open for her: she could, if she wished, change her status through penitence and redemption.

Jackie quickly spent money—about $1.5 million in the first year of their marriage—on clothes, travel, gifts, and redecorating the Skorpios house.

Aristotle was twenty-three years older than Jackie.

Strains in the marriage appeared when Ari returned to the arms of Maria Callas, and letters that Jackie had written to Roswell Gilpatric found their way into print. In addition, Jackie was seen in New York with other escorts. Onassis issued a public statement: "Jackie is a little bird that needs its freedom as well as its security, and she gets both from me. She can do exactly as she pleases—visit international fashion shows and travel and go out with friends to the theater or anyplace. And I, of course, will do exactly as I please. I never question her and she never questions me."

However, he secretly hired a lawyer and private

investigator to see if Jackie was indeed carrying on affairs. No evidence was found.

Nevertheless, Ari rewrote his will, granting his daughter, Christina, most of his estate, and leaving Jackie $250,000 (tax-free) a year, to be adjusted for inflation every three years. John and Caroline were to receive $50,000 of this amount until they were twenty-one. The will contained a stipulation that she would lose her allowance if she contested the will, and Onassis used his influence to get the Greek Parliament to pass laws preventing her from inheriting the 25 percent of his estate that Greek law reserved for widows.

Surprising everyone, he left half his estate to the establishment of a charitable foundation. This was very likely due to Jackie's influence.

By the time Ari was sent to the hospital in 1975 with gallstones, Jackie and Christina had stopped talking to each other. While visiting Ari, Jackie would speak to him in French while Christina spoke to him in Greek.

Ari died of bronchial pneumonia on March 15, 1975, in Paris, while Jackie was in New York. He was sixty-nine.

Jackie issued a statement to the press:

105

Aristotle Onassis rescued me at a time when my life was engulfed in shadows. He meant a lot to me. He brought me into a world where one could find both happiness and love. We lived through many beautiful experiences together which cannot be forgotten, and for which I will be eternally grateful. . . . Nothing has changed both with Aristotle's sisters and his daughter. The same love binds us as when he lived.

Senator Edward Kennedy accompanied Jackie to his funeral.

After an intense and emotional court battle with Christina Onassis, Jackie secured $26 million from Ari's fortunes, in a settlement in September 1977. Ari had reportedly offered only $3 million as a divorce settlement.

Preserving Culture and History

"I am passionate about architecture," Jackie once said. "We are the only country in the world that trashes its old buildings. Too late we realize how very much we need them."

As a trustee of the Municipal Art Society, Jackie

became a full-fledged activist. When she learned of plans to erect two towers, one of which was to be 925 feet high, at the southwest corner of Central Park, she became enraged at what she saw as the latest symptom of developer greed and excess. The traffic the structure would attract would clog the streets and dirty the air, and the shadows of the towers would darken much of Central Park. She took on one of the largest development partnerships in the city, Solomon Brothers and Mortimer B. Zuckerman's Boston Properties, and was so successful in applying legal and community pressure that the partners abandoned the project in 1993.

Although it was a designated landmark, the splendid Grand Central Terminal was threatened in 1968 by the owner of the terminal and a developer, who wanted to acquire rights to the "air space" above the terminal for a fifty-three-story office tower. Jackie became involved in 1977, taking her cause to the streets. Standing on a makeshift platform, she pleaded with passersby: "You must help me. This building is part of our heritage. It must not be deserted." She worked on the project full-time, and in 1978 the Supreme Court of the United States ruled that the terminal's air space must remain clear.

Two years later, Jackie learned of a proposal to

107

raze St. Bartholomew's Episcopal Church on Lexington Avenue and Fiftieth Street to make way for a fifty-nine story office tower. Jackie quickly mobilized and formed the Committee to Save St. Bartholomew's, which she cochaired with writer Brendan Gill. Jackie lobbied legislators and Governor Mario Cuomo to designate the church a landmark and spoke before a joint session of the New York Senate and Assembly: "The future of New York City is bleak if landmark laws no longer apply to religious institutions. I think that if you cut people off from what nourishes them spiritually or historically, then something inside of them dies." In 1991 the project was abandoned after the U.S. Supreme Court refused to hear the constitutional appeal of the developers.

Jackie sat on the advisory committee of the John F. Kennedy School of Government, which had taken on his name after his death. Sitting alongside ambassadors, cabinet members, and politicians, she was noted for her efforts to reach out to students, both on the committee and in the community.

In 1967, during a dinner conversation, Jackie learned of floods in Florence that threatened to destroy most of the treasured works of art kept there. Almost immediately she called Robert Kennedy to see what could be done through official channels, and was named honorary chairwoman of the Committee for the Rescue of Italian Art.

One of her unsuccessful projects was her involvement in attempting to save the eighty-three-year-old Metropolitan Opera House at Thirty-ninth Street and Broadway in New York.

After the death of Aristotle Onassis, Jackie was offered the post of New York City commissioner of cultural affairs by Edward I. Koch. Jackie respectfully declined the offer.

Jackie the Editor

For sixteen years leading up to her death, Jackie worked for Doubleday, first as an associate editor and later as a senior editor. She edited an average of twelve books a year throughout her career, specializing in history and the arts, and earning an annual salary of about $50,000.

She began her publishing career at Viking in 1975 after being approached for the position of consultant by Tom Guinzberg, a job that paid $200 a week. However, she resigned two years later after he published Jeffrey Archer's *Shall We Tell the President?*, a political thriller that contains an assassination attempt on

Edward Kennedy. *The New York Times* called the book "trash" and said that "anyone associated with such a publication should be ashamed of herself." Jackie sent a handwritten letter of resignation to Guinzberg, and issued a public statement:

> I tried to separate my lives as a Viking employee and a Kennedy relative. But this fall, when it was suggested that I had something to do with acquiring the book and that I was not distressed, I felt I had to resign.

Two compilations published by Viking bear her name as editor: *The Firebird and Other Russian Fairy Tales*, with illustrations by Boris Zvorykin, and *In the Russian Style*, with an introduction by Audrey Kennett and designed by Bryan Holme.

She edited a number of best-sellers, including *Moonwalk*, by Michael Jackson; *Dancing on My Grave*, by dancer Gelsey Kirkland; and *Healing and the Mind*, by Bill Moyers. Her other authors included Joseph Campbell, André Previn, Carly Simon (who wrote four children's books for Doubleday), and Martha Graham. However, her selections and interests ranged far from celebrities as well: before he was awarded the

Nobel prize, she introduced Egyptian writer Naguib Mahfouz to an American audience.

Her first novel acquired for Doubleday was *Call the Darkness Light,* by Nancy L. Zaroulis. She pushed hard for the acquisition and its promotion, and the book hit the best-seller lists in August 1979.

"I'm drawn to books that are out of our regular experience . . . other cultures, ancient histories," she told *Publisher's Weekly* in an interview. She went on to a revealing comment about her choice of a career: "One of the things I like about publishing is that you don't promote the editor—you promote the book and the author."

She got along well with co-workers in the crowded office, who soon accepted her as a "regular worker," attended office parties and picnics, regularly ate a light lunch of yogurt from home, fetched her own coffee, made her own trips to the Xerox machine, and was well respected for her abilities. She became known in the trade as "Doubleday's secret weapon" for her ability to draw high-profile authors.

Of course, Jackie could not ever be just another editor. Her assistant at Viking claims that she habitually shredded her memos to keep them from falling into the hands of trivia-seekers.

111

She worked with Jonathan Cott, a contributing editor at *Rolling Stone* and author of several books on Egypt, who had much to say about her abilities: "She had an incredible sense of literary style and structure. She was intelligent and passionate about the material; she was an ideal reader and an ideal editor."

Maurice Templesman

Jackie met Templesman in the late 1950s, when John Kennedy, then a U.S. senator, wanted to meet with representatives of the South African diamond business. It was Templesman, a powerful player in the African diamond business, who arranged the meeting. After Aristotle Onassis' death in 1975, Jackie and Templesman's friendship became close.

Maurice Templesman was born on August 26, 1929, in Antwerp, Belgium, to Orthodox Jewish parents. In 1940 the family escaped the Nazis and settled in the Upper West Side of Manhattan, and by the late forties he had joined his father's diamond business and married. In 1955 his father died, and he became a general partner in the family business.

Templesman left his wife in 1984, and although

they were never legally divorced, a get, or Orthodox Jewish divorce, was arranged. By 1988 he moved in with Jackie.

A shrewd investor, Maurice helped Jackie swell her fortune to an estimated $200 million. His advice was to buy gold options, which Jackie did in the seventies at about $100 an ounce. She was able to sell her option at over $800 an ounce in the early eighties.

As his diamond company, Leon Templesman & Son, is privately owned, no one knows Templesman's net worth.

He has been quietly appointed to several presidential commissions, including the President's Commission for the Observance of Human Rights, the Citizens' Advisory Board of Youth Opportunities, and the President's Council at the Center for International Studies at New York University.

In 1985, after he suffered a heart attack, Jackie visited him at Lenox Hill Hospital every day. After two weeks, he was released, and went to Jackie's apartment to recuperate.

Templesman kept his eighty-foot yacht, the *Relemar*, near Jackie's vacation home on Martha's Vineyard. When the Clintons visited Jackie in August

1993, she and Maurice took them on a long cruise on the *Relemar* with a crowd of Kennedys.

Templesman rarely left Jackie's side during her illness, and set up an office in her apartment to insure he would not have to.

VII

Taste and Style

Clothing

Jackie's first evening dress (blue taffeta, full-skirted, puff-sleeved) was donned for Shippen's 1942 Christmas party. She wore the dress with gold kid slippers.

Before moving to the White House, Jackie typically wore the work of European designers—Givenchy, André Courréges, Balenciaga, Yves Saint Laurent, Ungaro, Dior, Chanel—but realized, and was told, that as First Lady, she should wear American designs.

She discussed the importance of creating an "American look" with designer Oleg Cassini at their first meeting, as well as the hope that they together could give a boost to the American fashion industry.

In 1957 she and her sister posed for a fashion layout in *Ladies' Home Journal.* As they were both not yet as wealthy as they would become, they convinced the magazine to let them keep the clothes they wore for the shoot.

If Jackie had expensive tastes, she kept the bills to herself when talking to reporters. When interviewed for the 1957 *Ladies' Home Journal* article, she denied her avaricious appetite for apparel: "I don't like to buy a lot of clothes and have my closets full. A suit, a good little black dress with sleeves and a short evening dress—that's all you need for travel."

During the presidential campaign, she answered a question about her purchasing habits: "I'm sure I spend less than Mrs. Nixon on clothes. She gets hers at Elizabeth Arden, and nothing there costs less than $200 or $300."

Jackie was first named to Eleanor Lambert's International Best Dressed list in 1960, and reappeared on the list in 1961, 1962, and 1964.

Jack phoned Oleg Cassini to discuss her White House wardrobe while Jackie was still recovering from delivering John, Jr. He flew to Washington immediately and visited Jackie in the hospital. "You have an opportunity for an American Versailles," he told her, and offered to become her "design-courtier."

"She was under great pressure," Cassini remembers. "She had a lot of imagination and she was already thinking of her own responsibility, and she could not wait. She knew that no matter what the pressure of the moment, she had to think of tomorrow and of next week. She only had a few dresses. She knew that to have a decent wardrobe when she entered the White House, she had to think of it. And thus the new Jackie was an image in a way created by her and me."

Cassini drew upon his experiences of designing for film stars: "Suddenly it came to me. This is like a film and you have the opportunity to dress the female star. This was not so different from my old job in Hollywood."

Jack looked upon her dresses as an unnecessary expense, but his father, Joe, saw the importance of Jackie's public image and offered to pay for everything.

He wasn't just paying for a few dresses: Cassini hired a staff composed of a tailor, materials specialist, eight seamstresses, a live model who matched Jackie's measurements, and a contact in Europe who looked for unusual fabrics in France, Italy, and Switzerland. Cassini says that there were no limits placed on the amount he could spend on fabrics. "This was haute couture at its highest level," wrote Cassini.

Jackie's shoes were made by Eugenia of Florence, her handbags by Koret, and her hats and gloves by Bergdorf Goodman.

Jackie had already ordered a dress from Bergdorf Goodman in New York City for the inaugural ball, so she went ahead with her previous choice, but wore a Cassini dress to the gala organized by Frank Sinatra for the night before the inauguration. She called this dress her "favorite dress of all time." It was white, full-length, Swiss double satin, and very simple in design, with a small bow at the waist. The Goodman dress is on display at the Smithsonian Institution.

The Cassini dress Jackie wore to the inauguration itself was fawn-colored, made of soft wool, and accented with silk at the waistline and cuffs. It was to be worn with long black gloves, a pillbox hat, and a long coat with accents matching the dress and a sable collar. Jackie added a sable muff, which she already owned, to the ensemble. The large buttons on the coat would become a Jackie trademark, appearing on her informal dresses and coats throughout her stay at the White House.

In photographs, Jackie's outfit stands out from all

the other women at the event, who were wrapped deeply in fur. Jackie commented on this, saying, "I just didn't want to wear a fur coat. I don't know why, but perhaps because women huddling on the bleachers always looked like rows of fur-bearing animals."

Since Cassini agreed to work with Jackie under the condition that she would work with no one else, she had Bergdorf's send him her measurements, which were, for her dresses, as follows:

Bust 35½"; waist 26"; hips 38"; waistline to hem on side, 25½"; back of dress neck to waist 17½"; back of neck to floor 61"

Jackie's shape and features led Cassini's dresses in a direction inspired by military designs and hiero-glyphics. "I saw Jackie as a geometrical goddess," said Cassini.

Jackie's height was five feet seven and a half inches.

Jackie and Cassini conspired to take risks in her evening wear, but took matters slowly. Cassini tells a story of his first design that left Jackie's right shoul-der bare:

When I created a one-shouldered evening gown, Jackie loved it, but she was convinced her husband would not let her wear it. So I went to see the President. "From the dawn of antiquity, the queen or high priestess has always set the style. . . . I am proposing nothing outrageous or undignified; indeed the look is more than three thousand years old. The ancient Egyptians would have considered this dress rather conservative!

Jack agreed to the design while laughing over Oleg's impassioned plea. The liberation of one of Jackie's shoulders having met with success, Oleg later freed both shoulders simultaneously with a strapless evening gown.

Jackie wore one-shouldered "Nefertiti" gowns at the receptions for the president of Tunisia in 1961 and, later, for the president of Sudan.

Although she traveled to France in 1961 with a host of Cassini dresses and gowns, she wore a Givenchy gown to the state dinner at Versailles, for "political reasons."

Immediately a rumor started: Jackie's sister Lee was buying Givenchy designs and giving them to Cassini to imitate for Jackie. Jackie wrote Cassini a letter with advice on how to answer probing questions from the press.

When she met Khrushchev in Vienna, he was said to have remarked, "It's beautiful," referring, of course, to her shimmering pink-silver "mermaid" gown. He insisted on sitting next to her after dinner.

For her 1962 televised tour of the White House, Jackie wore a claret wool Cassini dress with a rounded neckline and a trompe l'oeil design that gave it the appearance of a two-piece. Large buttons, by now a trademark, added a contemporary feature.

To comply with Vatican protocol when visiting the pope, Jackie wore a full-length dress with full-length sleeves. Cassini made the dress from black silk, and Jackie borrowed a lace mantilla from her sister-in-law Ethel.

Once, in an attempt to shock her mother-in-law, she wore an outfit at lunch of strawberry linen shorts, a sleeveless yellow silk shirt, bright blue Capezio slippers with embroidered pearls, and a belt adorned with paintings of bats and inscribed "bats in your belfry."

According to designer Oleg Cassini, Jackie needed about three hundred dresses per year during her White House years.

In France, for her first meeting with de Gaulle, she won him over in part by wearing a white silk bell-skirted Hubert de Givenchy gown. After a trip to Versailles, the *France-Soir* honored her with the headline: "Apotheosis at Versailles: Versailles at last has a queen."

The fashion ripples set off in Paris traveled even deep beyond the Iron Curtain: the Polish magazine *Swiat* named her as one of the most influential women in setting the tone and style of the sixties, in the West and throughout the world.

Oddly, on the fateful day in Dallas, she did not wear a Cassini dress. The pink and navy Chanel-style suit was given to her by her sister.

For her wedding to Aristotle Onassis, Jackie wore a beige lace and chiffon dress from the Valentino collection. After her wedding, 36 brides immediately ordered the same dress, and 150 were sold in that year.

A photographer caught her in a surprising bikini held together by golden rings while she was on vacation with Onassis. Seeing the pictures in the paper, along with snide remarks in the captions, she realized this was probably a mistake, and it was not repeated.

For her White House portrait, Jackie wore a tea

gown of homespun wool by Irish designer Sybil Connolly.

For her job at Doubleday, she typically wore low-key silk shirts and pants. Black remained her color choice for formal evening wear, and Carolina Herrera designs for events.

For footwear, Jackie wore stacked, mid-high heels and, occasionally, flat-heeled Italian leather sandals with trousers. Her knee-high boots were acquired at Charles Jourdan, and she was often spotted buying shoes at Ferragamo. Once, reporters from a trade paper who were following her managed to catch a glimpse of her with a shoe off. They revealed her surprisingly large shoe size—ten—in their next issue.

The makers of Gloria Vanderbilt jeans once asked her to endorse a line of Jackie Jeans, but they received no reply.

Many of Jackie's clothes are now preserved at the Metropolitan Museum's Costume Institute.

According to her designer, Jackie's favorite color was white.

Jackie claimed that being a fashion icon was "at the very bottom of the list of things I desire."

Jewelry

Jackie's most spectacular pieces were made by David Webb, Kenneth Jay Lane, Van Cleef & Arpels, Cartier, Uri, Paget, and Lalaounis of Greece.

While in the White House, however, she appeared to prefer understated jewelry, such as her triple-strand pearls with art deco–style clasp. Both the pearls and the diamonds in the clasp were simulated.

Jackie often had jeweler David Webb design paperweights made of American minerals to give to visiting heads of state. King Hassan of Morocco was presented with a gold American eagle set in topaz.

Shortly before he was killed, Jack bought Jackie a ring with a forty-seven-carat cushion-shaped kunzite surrounded by four-carat diamonds mounted in eighteen-karat gold. He never got a chance to give her the ring.

The centerpiece of the engagement ring Aristotle Onassis gave Jackie was known as the Lesotho III Diamond. Weighing 40.42 carats, it was a piece of a larger 601-carat diamond discovered in May 1967 by Mrs. Ernestine Ramaboa in Lesotho, South Africa. Before it was cut in 1968 it was the eleventh largest diamond of gem quality and the largest ever discovered by a woman. The parent stone had been exhibited at the Smithsonian Institution in Washington, D.C., and the Museum of Natural History in New York before it was cleaved on live television by Pastor Colon.

His wedding presents included a ruby and diamond ring in a 17.68-carat ruby surrounded by 5.5-carat diamonds mounted on 18-karat gold and platinum, worth about $25,000; a diamond and emerald drop necklace with a total of 35 carats of diamonds and 132 carats of emeralds set in 18-karat gold from Van Cleef & Arpels, worth about $100,000; a pair of cabochon ear clips with 76-carat pear-shaped rubies surrounded by diamonds from Van Cleef & Arpels, at a cost of approximately $25,000; and a Van Cleef & Arpels necklace of cabochon rubies and emeralds with diamonds adding up to 47 carats and a pendant with a 56-carat ruby, worth approximately $85,000.

Aristotle showered a steady stream of jewelry on Jackie in their early marriage — an eighteen-karat gold, diamond, and stone bracelet worth $15,000 for an Easter present; a twenty-two-karat gold flower brooch bought for around $1,500; a ring with a single sixty-one-carat emerald in a ring of diamonds worth about $12,000 from Van Cleef & Arpels as a Christmas present.

To commemorate the moon landing in 1969, Ari

commissioned a pair of eighteen-karat gold and ruby ear clips for Jackie. Two spherical pieces of gold were hammered to resemble the moon and studded with rubies. The moons were suspended by a string of tiny gold space capsule replicas attached to tops that evoked a rocket in orbit. Greek actress Katina Paxinou complimented her earrings over dinner, and Jackie replied, "Ari was actually apologetic about them. He felt they were such trifles. But he promised me that if I'm good, next year he'll give me the moon itself."

Aristotle's family adorned Jackie as well. From his aunt she received a pair of eighteenth-century diamond chandelier earrings, and from her sister-in-law, a coral and diamond brooch and matching ear clips from Van Cleef & Arpels, Paris. The ear clips alone had 104 seven-carat diamonds, and the set was valued between $15,000 and $20,000.

Interior Design

After leaving the White House, Jackie called upon renowned designers such as Billy Baldwin, Harrison Cultra, Vincent Fourcade, John Fowler, Mark Hampton, and Richard Keith Langham to maintain her carefully chosen designs in her homes.

Her fifteen-room apartment at 1040 Fifth Avenue

covers the entire fourteenth floor. A small entrance foyer opens into a large gallery which connects to all the other rooms, radiating around it. The main living room is forty feet long and has spectacular views of Central Park. The apartment has five bedrooms, three servants' rooms, and a butler's pantry off the kitchen.

When she first moved in, she decorated the apartment with subdued, heavy, formal furniture, much like the White House she had recently left. In the 1990s she switched to French country, introducing lighter shades and a more casual atmosphere. Mahogany was replaced with fruitwood, the walls were washed to give the impression of stone, and some floors were done in terra-cotta tile. However, the completely white kitchen had never been redone.

In one corner of the living room, next to a window facing Central Park, stood an artist's drawing table where Jackie continued her lifelong love of painting and drawing.

In furniture she was drawn toward sturdier European designs rather than flamboyantly painted or primitive works. Strength was important: "John always tips back in his chair," she told one furniture expert on a shopping trip when she bought braced low-back Winsor chairs, passing over the delicate Sheraton comb-backs.

Photographs of John, John, Jr., and Caroline were present all over the apartment. In her bedroom is one photo of Onassis.

For her home in Martha's Vineyard, she spent $14,000 to buy and ship white oak for the hardwood floors. The opulent decks around the house were constructed from a ton of teak imported from Burma. She instructed that the windows not only look colonial, but be manufactured in the same way, with wooden pegs instead of nails and screws.

Portraits

The portrait of Jackie that hangs in the Vermeil Room of the White House was painted by Aaron Shikler, who also painted portraits of the Duchess of Windsor, Lauren Bacall, Joanne Woodward, Drue Heinz, Jane Engelhard, Annette de la Renta, and Brooke Astor. Jackie recommended Shikler for the portrait in 1967, after he completed a portrait of her children, and it was unveiled in 1971.

The official portrait, however, was not the original one. Shikler grew discontented with how this portrait was turning out, seeing in it too much melancholy for an official portrait. Also, while he was painting, Jackie became engaged to Aristotle Onassis, and the painter saw a change come over her: "She became jollier, gayer, much more relaxed and girlish." A lighter, more colorful approach was decided upon.

Art and Articles

Due to her intensive lobbying of Johnson, he founded the National Endowment for the Arts and Humanities.

With the backing of President Johnson, who was heavily influenced by Jackie, Congress approved a $17.5 million bill to build the John F. Kennedy Center for the Performing Arts, leaving the love and attention Jackie had for the arts a permanent home in Washington.

Jackie was on the American Ballet Theater's board of directors for twenty-five years.

Jackie said that the way to approach a piece of art is "by using your eyes, by focusing your whole attention on a work of art to try to understand the message the artist wants to convey."

Jackie and John F. Kennedy frequently exchanged gifts of Hellenistic statues, often bought from J.J.

Klejman, an antiquities store in New York City. Jackie continued to collect similar pieces while married to Aristotle Onassis. Among the pieces in her collection were a pair of Hellenistic terra-cotta horses from Canosa, third century B.C.; a Hellenistic marble torso of Aphrodite, second or first century B.C.; and a number of Roman bronze statues from the first to the third centuries B.C.

Jackie had a strong preference for French design of the eighteenth and nineteenth centuries, and perhaps her most striking piece was the pair of Louis XVI painted *fauteuils en cabriolet* owned by Thomas Jefferson. Jefferson bought the chairs when he was involved in trade negotiations in Paris between 1784 and 1789. The chairs, along with forty-four others and six sofas, were shipped to Monticello, his mansion in Charlottesville, after he became secretary of state, and were discovered in a Monticello loft in 1907. The chairs were sold after the estate changed owners and made their way into the Baltimore home of the Fisher family. Jackie bought the chairs in 1962.

They were likely a conversation piece at the 1962 White House dinner honoring forty-nine Nobel Laureates. President Kennedy called the group "the most extraordinary collection of talent, of human knowledge, that has ever been gathered at the White House, with the possible exception of when Thomas Jefferson dined alone."

Jackie consulted with interior designer Stéphan Boudin for the White House restoration, and acquired one of his carpet designs for the White House State Dining Room. The design was after the carpets Boudin had supplied to Lady Olive Baillie for the Leeds Castle dining room.

Jackie owned a number of pieces of fine natural history drawings from the collection of Lady Impey. Other examples of her collection can be found in England at the Victoria and Albert Museum and the Wellcome Institute.

Jackie also collected works of John Singer Sargent, including *Head of an Arab*, from his watercolor period of the early 1900s, and *Venetian Girl*, from one of his trips to Venice around that time. Another example of British watercolor in her collection was a John Ruskin painting of the Spanish Steps in Rome. Ruskin (1819–1900) was an extremely influential Victorian art critic as well as a painter.

Some of her French paintings were by Isidore Alexander Augustin Pils (1835–1875), who was at one time commissioned by Napoleon III, and highly respected landscape painter Charles-François Daubigny (1817–1878), whose work was praised by Corot, Rousseau, and Monet.

Jackie brought to the White House an impressive array of furnishings. One particularly spectacular piece was a restored parcel-gilded, brass-mounted and ebonized mahogany swivel-top card table, one of a group made by the School of Charles Honore Lannuier in New York, circa 1815. The table was one of a group, and the others can be found at the Albany Institute of History and Art and the Metropolitan Museum of Art.

Although she felt that rocking chairs were inappropriate for the White House ("A rocker is a rocker, and there isn't much you can do to make it look like anything else,"), she consented to include them in the Oval Office upon hearing from doctors that they could ease Jack's back pain.

Jackie's stay in the White House was the inspiration of many works of art, quite a few of which were given to Jackie herself. French artist Jacqueline Duhéme, a friend of Picasso, Matisse, and Eluard, presented Jackie with a watercolor-on-paper painting of her and her sister Lee riding a camel during their visit to Pakistan. Duhéme had been making "little doodles" of Jackie, which appeared in *Elle,* and when Jackie saw them, she invited the painter to the White House.

Painter Robert Rauschenberg honored the president and First Lady with *Drawing for the President of the USA with Dante,* a silkscreen drawing of iconocraphic images juxtaposed with drawings of Jack and Jackie, dated 1960.

Among the paintings Jackie hung in Jack's White House bedroom were two oil-on-canvas pieces of horses that were owned, along with their paintings, by Sir Charles Bunbury, founder of the Derby at Epsom and the 2,000 Guineas race.

Other important equestrian portraits in her collection were that of Peter the Great on a chestnut mare, painted by Nicolas-Louis-Albert Delerive, active from 1773 to 1806; and *Lord Bateman's Arabian,* by British painter John Wooton (1683–1764).

Continuing the tradition of each first family leaving a painting in the White House upon departure, Jackie chose a view of the Seine in Paris by Claude Monet and had it hung in the Green Room.

— JACKIE WITH MAURICE TEMPLESMAN —

VIII

An Untimely End

Diagnosis

Jackie noticed a swelling in her groin in November 1993, but the swelling responded to antibiotics. However, while on vacation in December, she reported flu-like symptoms to her doctor, including swelling in her glands and abdominal pain. Her doctor ordered her home immediately.

Jackie was diagnosed with non-Hodgkin's lymphoma in January 1994. She told Arthur Schlesinger, Jr., "I feel it is a kind of hubris. I have always been proud of keeping so fit. I swim and I jog, and I do my push-ups and walk around the reservoir, and I gave up smoking forty years ago. And now this suddenly happens."

When she told Maurice, he began to cry and called her children.

Non-Hodgkin's lymphoma strikes about forty-five thousand Americans each year; however, only about ten percent of the cases involve cancer cells as aggressive as the ones found in Jackie.

She publicly announced her diagnosis in February 1994. Her lifelong friend Nancy Tuckerman became her spokeswoman, and claimed that Jackie was responding well to the treatment.

Struggle for Life

As her cancer grew, she would arrive every two weeks at 7:00 A.M. at the office of an Upper East Side doctor for a CAT scan. Her head hidden by a hooded cape, she was always accompanied by Maurice, who checked the waiting room and sidewalk for reporters and photographers and carried a small sack with her breakfast.

Coping with the effects of the cancer and therapy with grace and humor came naturally to Jackie. Chemotherapy was not so bad, she told friends; she could read a book during the treatment. She had to undergo four courses of chemotherapy at the New York University–Cornell Medical Center.

She also attempted to cope with the illness using lessons she reaped from meditation and from her editorial work on Bill Moyers' book *Healing and the Mind*. Meditation helped her deal with chemotherapy's side effects and kept her calm and present.

The cancer in her body had initially responded to chemotherapy, which included use of steroids, but in March was found in her brain and throughout her abdomen. Radiation therapy was begun on her brain.

Doctors fought the cancer cells in her brain with a linear accelerator in the Stitch Radiation Therapy Center. The machine specialized in reaching cancer cells deep in the body, and it was not supposed to harm surrounding tissue. However, the months of chemotherapy had weakened her immune system, and she developed pneumonia. Doctors responded by prescribing huge doses of antibiotics.

Although doctors first told her that her cancer could be stabilized in 50 percent of cases, it was discovered in her liver on May 18, and doctors told her there was nothing more they could do. She left the hospital and requested the antibiotic treatment for her pneumonia be stopped. Her living will stated that no extraordinary measures were to be taken.

As her spokesperson, Nancy Tuckerman made the statement: "The disease has progressed. She will not have any further treatment. There was nothing more to do for her. She is very comfortable. She has her children around her, and that's the way it should be. How long it will go on, we don't know."

Final Days

Jackie gave confession and received the "Anointing of the Sick," a form of last rites that does not assume certain death, from Monsignor George Bardes of St. Thomas More Church while still lucid at home on May 19. A friend of the family said, "It was an issue for her and she made it clear she wanted to be conscious for her last rites."

Senator Edward M. Kennedy rushed from Washington to New York two nights in a row to stay by her bedside.

When word of her impending death got out, a mob of reporters from as far away as New Zealand gathered on her block on Fifth Avenue, unable to respect Jackie's final request for privacy. Eunice Kennedy Shriver was nearly hit by a bus while searching for a cab to escape the horde. Police eventually surrounded the apartment building with wooden barricades. One reporter, in a moment of self-reflection, called the gathering "ghoulish," and described himself and other reporters as "muggers."

140

Jackie Kennedy Onassis died at 10:15 P.M. on Thursday, May 19, 1994, "at home surrounded by her friends and family and her books, and the people and things she loved—in her own way, on her own terms," in the words of John F. Kennedy, Jr. He was at her bedside when she passed away, along with Caroline and Maurice. She was sixty-four. The exact cause of death was not released.

Outside her Fifth Avenue apartment, several hundred mourners gathered to leave flowers, scatter rose petals, and light candles. A wake was quickly arranged for family members on May 21 as her body lay in state inside the apartment.

Funeral and Burial

The private funeral was held at the church of Jackie's baptism and confirmation, St. Ignatius Loyola in New York, at 10:00 A.M. on May 23, 1994. A crowd of two thousand was held back by steel barricades during the eighty-minute service, which was attended by one thousand invited guests, including some of the most important people in politics, publishing, and entertainment—Hillary Clinton, Lady Bird Johnson, Yoko Ono, Daryl Hannah, Arnold Schwarzenegger, and Senators John Glenn, Daniel Patrick Moynihan,

John Kerry, and Claiborne Pell. Also on the list were some of those who perhaps knew Jackie's tastes best: Paul Madden, an antiques dealer, and her hairdresser of twelve years, Joseph Spadaro.

Reverend Walter Modrys officiated at the services at the church, located on Park Avenue and Eighty-fourth Street in Manhattan. Perhaps in honor of her childhood at that same church, he pronounced Jackie's name in the French style (zhak-leen), as she had originally preferred.

Teddy Kennedy, John, Jr., and Maurice Templesman offered their memories of Jackie:

No one else looked like her, spoke like her, wrote like her, or was so original in the way she did things. No one we knew ever had a better sense of self.

She lifted us up, and in the doubt and darkness, she gave her fellow citizens back their pride as Americans.

—SENATOR EDWARD M. KENNEDY

Choosing the readings for these services, we struggled to find ones that captured my mother's essence. Three things came to mind . . . and ultimately dictated our selections. They were her love of words, the bonds of home and family, and her spirit of adventure.

—JOHN F. KENNEDY, JR.

*But now the journey is over. Too short, alas too short.
It was filled with adventure and wisdom, laughter and
love, gallantry and grace. So farewell, farewell.*
                                    —MAURICE TEMPLESMAN

Templesman followed his eulogy by reading the
poem *Ithaka,* by the Greek poet C. P. Cavafy: "May
there be many a summer morning, when, with what
pleasure, what joy, you come into harbors seen for the
first time."

Caroline read the poem "Memory of Cape Cod,"
by Edna St. Vincent Millay, and soprano Jessye Norman sang Franck's "Panis Angelicus" and Schubert's
"Ave Maria."

No speaker at any time made reference to Jackie's
second marriage.

Her casket was dark mahogany, embellished with
greenery and baby's breath, arranged in the shape of
a cross, and a white pall draped over the top.

Although the Kennedy family made its customary
request for privacy, they allowed an audio feed to be
broadcast outside the church, which was broadcast live
by CBS, CNN, NBC, and hundreds of local stations.
ABC declined to cover the ceremony out of respect
for the family.

143

After the church service, the family flew to Washington by chartered jet with the casket, and met President Clinton at National Airport.

She was laid to rest at Arlington National Cemetery, next to the graves of John F. Kennedy, marked by the eternal flame she lit in 1963, the infant Patrick Bouvier Kennedy, and her unnamed stillborn daughter. Robert F. Kennedy's grave, marked by a simple white cross, is also nearby.

Honorary pallbearers were Robert F. Kennedy, Jr., Timothy Shriver, Christopher Lawford, William Kennedy Smith, Edward Kennedy, Jr., and Jack Walsh, the Secret Service agent who watched over John and Caroline in the White House. The casket, however, was carried by professional pallbearers.

"May the flame she lit, so long ago, burn ever brighter here and always brighter in our hearts," President Clinton said to the one hundred close friends, who were watched by a group of reporters gathered at a respectable distance. The Army Military District had distributed a warning to the media: "Those who try to penetrate the grave site area will be escorted out by law-enforcement officials."

Clinton praised her with the words: "She taught us by example about the beauty of art, the meaning of culture, the lessons of history, the power of personal courage, the nobility of public service, and most of all, the sanctity of family.

"She seemed always to do the right thing, in the right way."

Family friend and retired archbishop Reverend Philip M. Hannan, who had also performed services for John F. Kennedy, urged the group to pray for "the grace that will strengthen the bonds of family and of the national community," and remembered Jackie for her "life of endless love and light."

John, Jr., read from Thessalonians 4:13–18, and Caroline read Psalm 121.

Rose, then 103 years old, observed the ceremony by television from the Kennedy home in Hyannis Port.

The Navy Sea Chanters sang "Eternal Father," as they had thirty-one years before in honor of President Kennedy.

Twenty-three other funerals planned in Arlington that day went on as scheduled.

John Kennedy, Jr., who had saluted at his father's funeral in 1963, spontaneously leaned over to gently kiss the casket of his mother.

No relatives of the late Aristotle Onassis were in attendance.

The ceremony lasted only eleven minutes.

Far from the cemetery, the "passing" bell at the Gothic Washington National Cathedral rang sixty-four times, once for each year of her life.

Workers laid a headstone for Jackie in Arlington National Cemetery on October 7, 1994.

Only one other former First Lady is buried at Arlington National Cemetery: Mrs. William Howard Taft, who rests next to her husband.

The Will

Jackie made only two specific requests regarding her prized possessions: an ancient Hellenic marble head of a woman was to be given to Maurice Templesman, and two Indian miniature paintings to her friend Bunny Mellon. She also willed a copy of JFK's inaugural address with an inscription by Robert Frost to her lawyer, Alexander Forger.

Personal friends, maids, and the butler received cash gifts ranging from $25,000 to $250,000, with instructions that her estate would pay the taxes on these gifts.

To her children, Jackie left each $250,000 in cash,

the Fifth Avenue apartment, the Martha's Vineyard home, and the remainder of her belongings.

Jackie left the remainder of her estate to the C&J Foundation (C and J stand for the names of her children), a charitable trust designed to last twenty-four years. Caroline, John, Maurice Templesman, and Alexander Forger were named as trustees and directed to give annually eight percent of the value of the estate's assets to charities "committed to making a difference in the cultural or social betterment of mankind or the relief of human suffering." After twenty-four years, the assets will pass on to her grandchildren.

Her will also asks her children to keep her papers private.

The Auction

A total of 5,914 of Jackie's personal items were sold in a public auction at Sotheby's in Manhattan's Upper East Side from April 23 to 26, 1996. Sotheby's had estimated the total "fair market value," that is, the value the items would have had they not been owned by Jackie, at four million dollars. But when the final gavel fell, the sale had earned her children $34.5 million.

While several critics stepped forward to criticize

the children who would benefit from the sale, others close to Jackie maintained that it was her idea. "Jackie did mention in her will that the children, if they wanted to, should have an auction. She said that would be the practical thing to do," said Nancy Tuckerman, Jackie's White House social secretary and close friend. "She would say to me, 'I keep thinking about my children with all these things that have accumulated.'"

The catalog, which sold for $90 in hardcover and $55 in paperback, sold one hundred thousand copies before the auction. Proceeds from the catalog went to charities, including the John F. Kennedy Library Foundation, which received a total of one million dollars.

Buyers of the catalog were entered into a lottery to receive tickets to the exhibition, held at the Sotheby's New York City Gallery at 1334 York Avenue at Seventy-second Street over four days. Sotheby's realized they could only handle forty thousand at the exhibition, and those lucky enough to get tickets were assigned a date and time to arrive. All personal items — backpacks, strollers, umbrellas — had to be checked at the door, and photography was, of course, prohibited.

The top ten sellers in the auction were:

1. Jackie's engagement ring from Aristotle Onassis. Anthony J. F. O'Reilly, CEO of the H.J. Heinz Co., cast the winning bid of $2.6 million for Jackie's forty-carat diamond engagement ring given to her by Aristotle Onassis. Sotheby's had set its value at $500,000 to $600,000.

2. The Louis XVI desk upon which the Nuclear Test Ban Treaty of 1963 was signed. An anonymous European foundation paid $1,432,500 for this piece of history. The White House entered the bidding early, but quickly found that this item would never return to Washington.

3. John F. Kennedy's MacGregor Woods golf clubs. Clubs were sold with a red and black golf bag inscribed "JFK, Washington, DC," for $772,500 to Arnold Schwarzenegger, husband of JFK's niece Maria Shriver. Schwarzenegger also bought a Norman Rockwell painting of JFK for $134,500 and a leather desk set for $189,500.

4. John F. Kennedy's walnut cigar humidor. An intense bidding war erupted over the humidor given to JFK by Milton Berle. Marvin Shanken, publisher of *Cigar Aficionado,* who "didn't think about what it would cost," eventually paid $574,500. Berle, who had paid $800 for the humidor in 1961,

dropped out of the bidding at $180,000. The humidor's inscription reads: "To J.F.K. Good Health— Good Smoking, Milton Berle."

5. An oak rocking chair. The next-to-last item to be sold was this simple chair from Carolina Rocker, with caned backrest and loose back and seat cushions, which the president had used in the Oval Office. Singer Carole Bayer Sager bought the chair as a wedding present for her fiancé for $453,500.

6. An oak rocking chair. Rocking chairs were ubiquitous in Kennedy residences, as they helped John F. Kennedy ease his back pain. This chair, very similar to its slightly more expensive cousin, sold for $415,000.

7. Kunzite and diamond ring. The ring Jack bought for Jackie, but never gave her, was hammered up to $415,000. Sotheby's had set its value at between $6,000 and $8,000.

8. Set of Ben Hogan Power Thrust irons. The golf clubs came with a black leather MacGregor tourney bag, inscribed "JFK, Washington, DC." Their market value was between $700 and $900.

9. Cabochon ruby and diamond pendant ear clips. While the market value was set at $25,000 to

$35,000, the fact that these were a wedding present from Ari to Jackie made them a must-have for several buyers. The end result: $360,000.

10. John Wooton oil painting of *Lord Bateman's Arabian*. Wooton was the most important landscape and sporting painter in Britain in the early eighteenth century, but the market value of this piece was no more than $120,000. Jackie's ownership brought the price up to $343,500.

Lot number one was a pair of engravings of seashells, valued at around $600. The bidding quickly went up to $6,900 an the crowd fell silent, probably taking this as an omen and refiguring their bids on items to come.

Singer Jimmy Buffett secured a Jamie Wyeth lithograph of the president in a sailboat for $43,700 and a copy of the first edition of the Short-Title List of the White House Library inscribed by Lady Bird Johnson.

Jackie's engraved sterling silver Tiffany tape measure, deemed to be worth $500 to $700, was taken by Manhattan interior designer Juan Molyneux on the auction's first day for $48,875.

Jackie's triple strand of fake pearls was valued at $700 to $900, but was eventually sold to the owners of the Franklin Mint Museum for $211,500. The Franklin Mint now sells replicas of the necklace, made of 139 European glass pearls color-matched to the originals, for $195.

Jackie had received two gold commemorative charms for her role as matron of honor at the launching of the carrier *John F. Kennedy, CVA-67* at Newport News on May 26, 1967. They were sold for $31,625.

One seeming "bargain" in the sale was a set of twelve Wedgwood creamware dinner plates, sold for $5,000 to Los Angeles attorney Ronald Palmieri.

The least expensive lot was a set of six books from Jackie's library, which went to a Florida dentist for $1,250.

The White House itself was represented at the auction, apparently trying to claim back some of Jackie's personal items that graced the house for her brief stay. Using private donations, it made just one purchase: an original drawing of a reception in the Blue Room in 1860, during the administration of President James Buchanan, for $14,000.

A model of Air Force One, valued at $500, opened

for bidding at $10,000, and after it sold for $42,500, the audience erupted into applause and laughter.

Comedian Joan Rivers "accidentally" won the bidding for a nineteenth-century French painting, *A Park View*, which had hung in the White House West Sitting Room, at $13,800. "I didn't realize my hand was up," she claimed. "I have a *painting.*"

Two women, one from North Carolina and one from South Carolina, who had traveled separately to the auction and were frustrated, outbid strangers on the first day, met and decided to pool their resources to get a winning bid. The pair paid $3,000 for a set of eight Chinese and Japanese porcelain dishes. Other bidders applauded as the women laughed and screamed over their victory.

Caroline's old rocking horse sold for $85,000.

The most overvalued item was a nineteenth-century gouache of an Indian ruler, which sold for $23,000 and was estimated high by $7,000.

The last item to be sold was Jackie's 1992 BMW 325i sedan, which fetched $79,000.

Not a single item went unsold.

Fifty-nine lots sold for more than one hundred times the high market value Sotheby's had estimated. Of the twenty items that went for the most over their estimate, six were golf equipment, four were jewelry, three had Jackie's monogram, and two were photos of drawings.

A New York magazine figured out that items the Kennedys definitely sat in—the rocking chairs, Jackie's saddles, Caroline's toy horse, John, Jr.'s high chair—went for an average of 101.8 times the high estimates. The overall average was 23.34 times the high estimate, or an average of $57,500.

The auction was Sotheby's seventh largest, the largest being the 1989 auction of the collection of Campbell Soup heir John Dorrance, which brought in $135 million.

The amount spent at the auction brought to light other, smaller collections of Kennedy and Jackie memorabilia which will, according to their holders, never be sold. At Miss Porter's School in Farmington, Connecticut, a small collection of Jackie's former items will be kept to "pass on to the next generation," according to Carol Messineo, the school's public relations director.

Jackie's copy of *A Complete Treatise on the Conjugation of French Verbs* from her days at Farmington sold at the auction for $42,550.

The bidders at the Sotheby's auction will therefore

never get a chance at a stuffed elephant with the name "Jacqueline Bouvier" stitched on the back, the handwritten copy of a speech "Be Kind and Do Your Share," original drawings for the school paper, a silver cup for a horsemanship competition, and a copy of a yearbook signed by Jackie.

Robert White of Catonsville, Maryland, has been collecting JFK items for thirty years, and estimates he owns over one hundred thousand pieces. These include Kennedy's black alligator-skin Hermès briefcase, a passport from his Senate days, and a money clip he was carrying in Dallas.

Some documents include his first Washington address book, and pages of notes and doodles, one of which has a brief reminder: "blockade Cuba," with a box drawn around the name of Fidel Castro.

White claims he obtained the items from a "source" in the White House, who started sending unwanted and unclaimed pieces to him after the assassination. White has no intention of selling the collection, and has approached the city of Annapolis with the idea of building a museum.

© Globe Photos, Inc.

IX

In Memory

Within a year of her death, New York City renamed the Central Park Reservoir, where she liked to jog and bicycle, the Jacqueline Kennedy Onassis Reservoir, and the Midtown High School for International Careers was renamed to honor her memory, a change initiated by students of the school.

The site of her and Jack's graves at Arlington National Cemetery attracts four million visitors per year, more than any other site in the cemetery.

Hammersmith Farm is now a museum called "Summer White House," run by a company named Camelot Gardens.

The Republic of Chad issued a set of nine commemorative stamps of Jackie after her death. One shows her in her first wedding dress, another in her trademark pillbox hat. They are worth two hundred francs of postage.

Within a year of her death, Jackie's grave site had acquired mystical powers. "Doctors Baffled as Hundreds Get Well — Instantly! Jackie Kennedy's Grave Heals the Sick!" announced one tabloid headline. "When I got there I felt my craving for heroin leave me," proclaimed one former drug addict.

The John F. Kennedy Memorial Library

Jackie was instrumental in the development of the John F. Kennedy Memorial Library, and helped choose I. M. Pei as its architect. A letter to him, carved in stone, stands at the entrance. "I have done my duty to your memory," it reads. "I respect your loneliness and solitude, which I share."

Perhaps one of the most valuable recordings in existence is Jackie's twelve-hour oral history, which she made herself after the assassination, now hidden away in the archives of the John F. Kennedy Memorial Library. It will not be released until 2044, fifty years after her death.

These tapes, together with the tapes of the interview given to William Manchester, insure that Jackie will be an endless source of fascination to biographers and historians of future generations.

Excluded from the sale by Jackie's children and

donated to the John F. Kennedy Memorial Library in Boston were: Jackie's first wedding dress, the diamond and emerald engagement ring given to Jackie by JFK, the maroon suit worn by Jackie while conducting her televised tour of the White House, a gold ring bearing the Kennedy crest with the engraving "May 29, 1961" (a birthday gift from the First Lady to the president), and a pair of trompe l'oeil painted doors Jackie installed on a cabinet in her dressing room in the White House. On the doors are depicted photographs, books, art, and objects of special meaning to her.

Jewelry given to the library included a gold, diamond, enamel, ruby, emerald, and aventurine belt and bracelet from Morocco and a suite of gold jewelry from Mexico comprising three necklaces and five brooches in Aztec design.

Among the works of art given to the museum were a charcoal sketch of John F. Kennedy by Elaine de Kooning, one of a series undertaken in late December 1962 and early January 1963 at Palm Beach in preparation for a formal portrait commissioned by the Truman Library but never completed, watercolor renderings by Edward Lehman depicting the White House Blue Room and Green Room as restored by Jacqueline

159

Kennedy, and an oil sketch of Jackie by Aaron Shikler, a preliminary study for her official White House portrait.

Several important documents were granted to the library, including copy number one of a limited first edition of one hundred of *The White House: An Historic Guide,* bound in leather and autographed by John F. Kennedy and Jackie, and a copy of the 1961 publication *The Jerusalem Windows,* by Marc Chagall, inscribed "to President Kennedy" by Chagall with an ink and watercolor drawing of the artist at work.

Personal papers donated to the library included those of 1991–1993 on the Bouvier family, papers relating to her childhood, trip files, records of Jackie's historic preservation projects in Washington and New York, including restoration of the White House, social records of the White House period, oral history interviews, personal correspondence, mail on the death of President Kennedy, correspondence relating to the establishment and construction of the Kennedy Library, and President Kennedy's personal copy of the Limited Nuclear Test Ban Treaty of 1963.

Photographs given the library include those of the restoration of the White House, the establishment of the White House Rose Garden, acquisition of objects for the White House Collection, and Jacqueline Kennedy's activities as First Lady.

Altogether, Jackie's children gave the library over thirty-eight thousand pages of documents, forty-five hundred photographs, and two hundred artifacts and works of art.

In May 1995 the John F. Kennedy Memorial Library released the full thirty-four pages of Jackie's last interview before beginning her private life, with Theodore H. White for *Life*, which included White's notes and revisions in Jackie's handwriting. White had donated the papers to the Library in 1969, under the condition that they remain closed until a year after Jackie's death.

New to the public were comments such as:

"When this is over, I'm going to crawl into the deepest retirement there is."

"I want John-John to be a fine young man. He's so interested in planes; maybe he'll be an astronaut or just plain John Kennedy fixing planes on the ground."

On Caroline: "She held my hand like a soldier. She's my helper, she's mine now."

On remembering her husband: "I wanted the flame and I wanted Cape Kennedy. . . . All I wanted was his name on just one booster, the one that would put us ahead of the Russians."

She had mentioned how she wanted to go back to the house in Georgetown they occupied before the presidency. "But then I thought, how can I go back there to that bedroom? I said to myself, you must never forget Jack, but you mustn't be morbid."

The typescript also reveals her insistent promotion of the idea of "Camelot." Where White first has her quoting the song, she added: "and it will never be that way again!" At the end of the interview she wrote: "And all she could think of was 'tell people there will never be that Camelot again.'"

Tributes

If she taught us anything, it was to know the meaning of responsibility—to one's family and to one's community. Her great gift of grace and style and dignity and heroism is an example that will live through the ages.

—HILLARY CLINTON

It leaves an empty place in the world as I have known it. We shared a unique time and I always thought of her as my friend.

—LADY BIRD JOHNSON

Jimmy and I were touched by the delightful and gracious atmosphere that Jacqueline Kennedy Onassis created in the White House. The charm of each room has been permanently enhanced as a result of her contributions.

—ROSALYNN CARTER

She was very kind to me when my husband was shot, and when we didn't know whether he was going to live or not. . . . She wrote me a very sweet, sensitive note and called me. . . . She couldn't have been nicer to me at that time when I really needed it.

—NANCY REAGAN

Jacqueline Kennedy Onassis was a model of courage and dignity for all Americans and all the world. Even in the face of impossible tragedy, she carried the grief of her family and our entire nation with a calm power that somehow reassured all of us who mourned. More than any other woman of her time, she captivated our nation and the world with her intelligence, elegance, and grace.

—BILL CLINTON

Jackie Onassis brought great dignity and grace to the White House and was indeed a charming and wonderful first lady.

—GEORGE BUSH

163

Her presence was evident in the warmth of every room and the charm of every hall [of the White House]. Clearly, her beautification efforts will be one of her enduring legacies.

—RONALD REAGAN

She showed us how one could approach tragedy with courage.
—JIMMY CARTER

America lost a heroine and I lost a friend.
—SENATOR JOHN GLENN

I think that after Eleanor Roosevelt, First Ladies were invisible. Women, in general, weren't very visible. Then, when Jackie burst on the scene, she made women visible again—in the public eye and in the new medium of television. And she was talented and accomplished in her own right as well as being her husband's partner.

—SENATOR BARBARA MIKULSKI

Few Americans ever received more public and media attention in their adult life than Jacqueline Kennedy Onassis. And few Americans ever handled that attention with as much dignity and grace as Mrs. Onassis.

—SENATOR BOB DOLE

Jacqueline Kennedy Onassis combined intellectualism with social tradition—professionalism with style and grace—and created, perhaps ahead of her time, a standard for contemporary American women.

—REPRESENTATIVE THOMAS FOLEY

Jackie was our bright shining star—a First Lady who lifted our spirits and made us love life more. . . . I seldom saw her or thought of her without experiencing the inward smile that is the gift of a genuine spirit. I shall always be proud to have become her friend.

—GEORGE MCGOVERN

She will be remembered with great affection and admiration by Irish people everywhere.

—MARY ROBINSON, President of Ireland

We remember the tragic image of the young widow at the funeral and her remarkable dignity and composure. She will always be remembered for that courage.

—ANATOLY KRASIKOV, deputy spokesman
for Russian President Boris N. Yeltsin

She was a classy young lady. Perhaps her greatest contribution was getting this country through those three or four days. I'm not so sure I could have done it without her. She was thirty-five [when Kennedy was assassinated]. She found an inner strength at a time in her life when most people haven't had to prove themselves at much of anything.

— BEN BRADLEE, SR., friend and former
Washington Post executive editor

She was extremely kind. In the two days after John Kennedy was assassinated, she gave every counselor to the president a private present, something she'd taken out of Jack's files or something. She gave me this wonderful leather thing, two cigars I can put into it, and on it, it says "JFK." She wanted me to remember that.

— PIERRE SALINGER, Kennedy press secretary

She changed the view of the First Lady. As someone said, she was the first one who didn't look like your grandmother. I think what probably will be remembered is dignity, privacy, class, as in high class; high style, not just fashion or decoration, but the way she lived. We haven't seen her for over thirty years really in any TV interview, no posed picture for thirty-one years, and yet

she is probably the best-known woman in the world. She did that by holding herself aloof and leading her own life.
  —FRANK MANKIEWICZ, Robert Kennedy's
    press secretary

Her greatest legacy is the impact of a caring mother on her children, Caroline and John. They are the finest examples of a widowed parent who kept her children on an even keel despite the terrible trauma of their father's death, all the national attention and curiosity they had to deal with. They were the greatest rewards of her lifetime.
  —JOHN T. FALLON, family friend and
    chairman and CEO of R.M. Bradley & Co.

The way she assumed the duties of the widow of an assassinated president so bravely and so intelligently is what really made her. Majesty is not the right word. She had poise. She demonstrated what a widow can do to heal the wounds of a country.
  —SAMUEL HUTCHINSON BEER, political scientist,
    professor emeritus, Harvard University

What she did for her country in the four dark days after her husband's assassination and especially during the fu-

neral made her a heroine for the ages. Not Joan of Arc, not Guinevere herself, ever showed greater nobility.

—DAN RATHER

She was as witty, warm, and creative in private as she was grand and graceful in public.

—BILL MOYERS

I admire most the way she evolved as a woman. Imagine being married to Jack Kennedy, with all that energy and charisma! People forget how young she was, too. As unofficial White House curator, she managed to turn a fusty old mansion into a beautiful museum, besides being both wife and mother. In that sense Jackie was way ahead of her time. She evolved in a way that any self-respecting feminist would consider brilliant: raised her children, had a successful publishing career, devoted herself to her grandchildren. Yet here is a woman who lost a baby and a husband in the space of three months.

—SALLY QUINN, author

She obviously had considerable talent, considerable ambition, and brains. You have to see her life as a significant and poignant mark in the evolution of women. She was the beautiful, sad heroine of our time.

—BETTY FRIEDAN

*She became a modern pop icon at a time when the media
was growing bigger, period. With her came the advent of
the paparazzi, and because the best shots of her captured
Jackie in motion—on a sailboat, riding a horse—she
transformed the fashion photography industry by giving
it a sense of youthfulness and motion it never had before.
Later, in New York, it was a given that if you got Jackie
Onassis on your fund-raising committee, the event was a
sellout. A done deal. Nobody else in the city had that
clout.*

—BILLY NORWICH, *Vogue* editor at large

*Her type of celebrity is something we'll probably never
see again. When you look at who we have for celebrities
today—Madonna, Roseanne—it doesn't take a genius to
see a kind of de-evolution there. What endeared me to
Jackie was that she never went on the couch with Barbara
Walters, talking about chemical dependency or incest or
whatever. It was her gift to us in many ways. It preserved
her sense of mystery.*

—GIP HOPPE, playwright, *Jackie: An American Life*

*Jack Kennedy once looked around a roomful of Nobel
Prize winners and called it the greatest collection of talent
in the White House since Thomas Jefferson dined alone.*

169

Well, Jackie was part of that feeling. She brought Pablo Casals and André Malraux to the White House, among many others. In New York she was enormously influential in saving Grand Central Station. She also edited two of my books. . . . One thing abut having Jackie as an editor, she could pick up the telephone and get absolutely anyone in the world on the line.

—George Plimpton, author

She was a last link to a certain kind of past, and that is part, but only part, of why we must mourn so. Jackie Kennedy symbolized—she was a connection to a time, to an old America that was more dignified, more private, an America in which standards were higher and clearer and elegance meant something, a time when elegance was a kind of statement, a way of dressing up the world, and so a generous act.

—Peggy Noonan

With her grace, charm, and elegance, Jacqueline Kennedy Onassis captivated the world like no other woman of her time. She epitomized fashion and style in America and was copied by millions of women around the world. Her contribution to fashion was to introduce naturalness to elegance.

—Carolina Herrera, designer

170

A woman of extremely good taste, a marvelous influence in the arts, in furniture, in food and in clothes. . . . She did not want to appear to be madly obsessed by fashion. She created fashion because she was who she was. But she did not want to appear to be the darling of the fashion world.

—OLEG CASSINI

She looked like a starlet who would never learn to act.
—NORMAN MAILER

You could hear her name in the air: Jackie, Jackie. There's so much awe and respect. Being with her is like walking with a saint.

—ANDY WARHOL

Bibliography

Adler, Bill, ed. *The Uncommon Wisdom of Jacqueline Kennedy Onassis.* New York: Citadel Press, 1994.

Allen, Henry. "Appreciation; Jackie Kennedy Onassis, an American Enigma; the Woman We Watched Endlessly but Never Saw." *Washington Post,* 20 May 1996, C1.

American Medical News. "Patients Ask: 'If Jackie Had a Living Will, Shouldn't I'?" *American Medical News,* 13 June 1994, 24.

Andersen, Christopher. *Jack and Jackie: Portrait of an American Marriage.* New York: William Morrow and Company, Inc., 1996.

Apple, R. W. "Death of a First Lady: The Overview." *New York Times,* 24 May 1994, A1.

Associated Press. "Hundreds Gather to Pay Respects to Jackie Kennedy." *Toronto Star,* 22 May 1994, A14.

Associated Press. "Jackie Kennedy: Seeking Privacy; in '63 Interview, She Also Wanted Memorials for JFK." *Chicago Tribune*, 28 May 1995, 10C.

Atlanta Constitution. "Jacqueline Kennedy Onassis 1929–1994." *Atlanta Constitution*, 24 May 1994, A6.

Atlanta Journal and Constitution. "Jacqueline Kennedy Onassis: 1929–1994." *Atlanta Journal and Constitution*, 20 May, 1994, A1.

Atlanta Journal and Constitution. "Remembering Jacqueline Kennedy Onassis." *Atlanta Journal and Constitution*, 21 May 1996, A14.

Baer, Susan. "Jacqueline Kennedy Helped Define the Terms History Uses about JFK." *Baltimore Sun*, 27 May 1995, 1E.

Boston Globe. "Words of Tribute at Cemetery, Church." *Boston Globe*, 24 May 1994, News 1.

Boston Herald. "Jacqueline Kennedy Onassis, 1929–1994; Unflappable Jackie Captured the World." *Boston Herald*, 29 May 1994, News 16.

Broder, David. "Jacqueline Kennedy's Legacy of Service." *Denver Post*, 24 May 1994, B7.

Brooks, Diana D., president and CEO, Sotheby's. Letter, 5 March 1996.

Buck, Genevieve. "Jackie Kennedy Onassis' Elegance

Set and Transcended Fashion." *Chicago Tribune,* 22 May 1994, Tempo 1C.

Burns, Carole. "At Miss Porter's School, Miss Bouvier Is Just Not for Sale." *New York Times,* 27 April 1996, Metro 26.

Burns, David (AP). "Two heroes for Our Time Put Others First." *Chicago Sun-Times,* 24 May 1994.

Bynum, Chris. "Camelot's Queen Reigned in Style." *The Times-Picayune,* 26 May 1994, E1.

Cassini, Oleg. *A Thousand Days of Magic: Dressing Jacqueline Kennedy for the White House.* New York: Rizzoli, 1995.

Cerio, Gregory, Sabrina McFarland, Allison Lynn, Alicia Brooks, and Stephen Sawicki. "Life without Jackie." *People,* 29 May 1995, 48.

Cleveland Plain Dealer Editorial. "Jacqueline Kennedy Onassis." *Cleveland Plain Dealer,* 22 May 1994, 2C.

Collier, Peter, and David Horowitz. *The Kennedys: An American Drama.* New York: Warner Books, 1984.

Collins, Amy Fine. "JKO; Tribute to the Fashion Style of Jacqueline Kennedy Onassis." *Harper's Bazaar,* August 1994, 148.

Dallas Morning News Editorial. "First Lady, Jacqueline Kennedy Onassis Set Style for Nation." *Dallas Morning News,* 21 May 1994, Editorials, 30A.

Dames, Joan Foster. "To the Manner Born; Jackie Kennedy's Right Hand Woman Brings Etiquette up to Date." *St. Louis Post-Dispatch,* 29 June 1995, Style West 1.

David, Lester. *Jacqueline Kennedy Onassis: A Portrait of Her Private Years.* New York: Birch Lane Press, 1994.

Dobell, Byron. "The Forgotten Portrait." *Town & Country,* July 1995, 74.

Douglas, William. "Jacqueline Kennedy Onassis—A City Mourns; Glamour with a Capital 'G.'" *New York Newsday,* 21 May 1994, A6.

Fainaru, Steve, and Michael Kranish. "Onassis to Be Buried Monday." *Boston Globe,* 21 May 1994, National/Foreign 1.

Fee, Gayle, and Laura Raposa. "Jacqueline Kennedy Onassis 1929–1994; Vineyard Loved Graceful Lady." *Boston Herald,* 20 May 1994, News, 8.

Filler, Martin. "1,200 Lots of Camelot." *House Beautiful,* April 1996, 72.

Filler, Martin. "Jackie, Queen of Arts." *House Beautiful,* September 1994, 90.

Fiori, Pamela. "In Loving Memory." *Town & Country,* July 1994, 46.

Gelzinis, Peter. "Jacqueline Kennedy Onassis,

1929–1994; in the Middle of the Circus Stood Some Who Really Cared." *Boston Herald*, 20 May 1994, News 22.

Gleick, Elizabeth. "The Man Who Loved Jackie." *People*, 11 July 1994, 74.

Goodman, Ellen. "Jackie Kennedy: Former First Lady Stayed True to Self." *Dallas Morning News*, 22 May 1994, 5J.

Gordy, Molly. "Jacqueline Kennedy Onassis: A City Mourns." *Newsday*, 21 May 1994, A5.

Gray, Christopher. "Streetscapes: Jacqueline Kennedy Onassis' Grandfather; Quality Developer with a Legacy of Fine Buildings." *New York Times*, 12 March 1995, section 9, p. 6.

Gray, Paul. "What Price Camelot?; an Auction of Jackie Kennedy's Personal Belongings Draws Throngs Eager to Pay a Premium for History." *Time*, 6 May 1996, 66.

Hanchette, John. "Jacqueline Kennedy Onassis/ 1929–1994." *USA Today*, 20 May 1994, 1A.

Hegarty, Trish. "Non-Hodgkin's Lymphoma is Often Treatable for Years." *Irish Times*, 23 May 1994, 4.

Heymann, C. David. *A Woman Named Jackie*, complete and updated edition. New York: Birch Lane Press, 1994.

Hohler, Bob. "Arlington Site for Onassis Prepared." *Boston Globe*, 22 May 1994, National/Foreign 20.

Hohler, Bob, and Steve Fainaru. "Farewell to a Lady." *Boston Globe*, 24 May 1994, 1.

International Collectors Society. Advertisement, *New York Post*, 8 July 1996.

Janofsky, Michael. "JFK Trove Available for Love, not Money." *New York Times*, 24 May 1996, A12.

John F. Kennedy Library Foundation. Press release, 19 June 1996.

Johnson, Marylin. "Dixie Style; Mother of all Pearls." *Atlanta Constitution*, 30 June 1996, 8M.

Johnson, Marilyn. "Her Own Woman: An Appreciation of Jacqueline Bouvier Kennedy Onassis." *Life*, July 1994, 48.

Kahn, Joseph P., Chris Black, and Michael Kranish. " 'It Leaves an Empty Place.' " *Boston Globe*, 21 May 1996, National/Foreign 6.

King, Larry. *Larry King Live, 28 March 1996.* Washington, D.C.: Cable News Network, 1996. Television broadcast.

Koestenbaum, Wayne. *Jackie Under My Skin.* New York: Plume, 1996.

Kuhn, Susan E. "Lessons from the Will of Jacqueline Kennedy Onassis." *Fortune*, 11 July 1994, 23.

Latham, Caroline, and Jeannie Sakol. *The Kennedy Encyclopedia*. New York: New American Library, 1989.

Leamer, Laurence. *The Kennedy Women*. New York: Ballantine, 1994.

Leigh, Wendy. "Caroline's Precious Legacy." *McCall's*, September 1994, 114.

Leithauser, Tom. "$7,000 Box to Hold His Toothbrush." *Orlando Sentinel*, 26 April 1996, A13.

Lunn, Judy. "A Last Few Words on Jacqueline Kennedy Onassis." *Houston Post*, 26 May 1994, H5.

Matthews, Christopher. "Best of Royalty in Jacqueline Kennedy." *Houston Chronicle*, 21 May 1994, A30.

McFadden, Robert. "Death of a First Lady." *New York Times*, 20 May 1994, A1.

McGory, Brian. "Jacqueline Onassis' Death Closes Chapter on Camelot." *Boston Globe*, 22 May 1994 National/Foreign 1.

Min, Janice et al. "Camelot by the Lot." *People*, 6 May 1996, 46–51.

Modrys, Walter F. "Jacqueline Kennedy Onassis; in Memoriam; Text of Homily of Burial Mass, May 23, 1994." *America*, 18 June 1994, 4.

Nadelson, Regie. "Jacqueline Kennedy Onassis." *The Independent*, 21 May 1994, 12.

New York Magazine. "The Price of Jackie's Fame, to the Last Penny." *New York,* 13 May 1996, 16.

New York Newsday. "Jacqueline Kennedy Onassis — A City Mourns; Kind Words at a Rough Time." *New York Newsday,* 21 May 1994, A6.

Noonan, Peggy. "America's First Lady." *Time,* 30 May 1994, 22.

O'Clery, Conor. "Jacqueline Kennedy Onassis." *The Irish Times,* 21 May 1994, News Features 6.

O'Connor, Coleen. "Jacqueline Kennedy Onassis dies at 64." *Dallas Morning News,* 20 May 1994, 1A.

Orlando Sentinel Tribune. "Last Rites for Jackie Kennedy Onassis." *Orlando Sentinel,* 20 May 1994, A1.

Page, Tim. "Jacqueline Kennedy Onassis — A City Mourns; Patron of Classical Music." *New York Newsday,* 21 May 1994, A11.

People magazine. "Together, Side by Side." *People,* 24 October 1994, 111.

Petkanas, Christopher. "Dearest Sister . . . Love Jackie." *Chicago Tribune,* 7 January 1996, N1.

Philp, Richard. "Kickoff: Tribute to the Late Jacqueline Kennedy Onassis, Her Contribution to 1960s Culture and the Creation of Robert Joffrey's Ballet 'Astarte' During That Era; Editorial." *Dance Magazine,* August 1994, 5.

Publishers Weekly. "Jacqueline Kennedy Onassis, Obituary." *Publishers Weekly,* 23 May 1994, 32.

Pye, Michael. "Jacqueline Kennedy Onassis Served her Country in an Extraordinary Way." *The Scotsman,* 21 May 1994.

Rogers, Patrick, and Maria Speidel. "Joan Rivers Reports from the Front Lines." *People,* 6 May 1996, 51.

Saltus, Richard. "Swift End No Surprise to Cancer Specialists." *Boston Globe,* 21 May 1994, National/Foreign 6.

Sapsted, David. "Jacqueline Kennedy's Lover Dies." *Daily Telegraph,* 20 March, 1996, 13.

Schlesinger, Arthur M., Jr. "Why We Mourn the Passing of Jacqueline Kennedy." *Dallas Morning News,* 23 May 1994, 13A.

Scott, Dale. "Jacqueline Kennedy Onassis—A City Mourns; Dying with Dignity." *New York Newsday,* 21 May 1994, A6.

Shribman, David. "Rites Provide Warmest Way to Remember." *Boston Globe,* 24 May 1994, 1.

Siegel, Ed. "Jacqueline Bouvier Kennedy Onassis 1929–1994: The TV Coverage." *Boston Globe,* May 24, 1994, 13.

Sotheby's. *The Estate of Jacqueline Kennedy Onassis.* New York: Sotheby's, 1996.

Star-Tribune. "Far Exceeding Sotheby's Wildest Dreams . . ." *Star Tribune,* 27 April 1996, 8A.

Sullivan, Paul, and Joe Heaney. "Jacqueline Kennedy Onassis 1929–1994; Camelot's Last Symbol Is Gone." *Boston Herald,* 20 May 1994, News, 4.

Times Newspapers Limited. "Jacqueline Kennedy Onassis." *The Times,* 21 May 1994, Features.

Times Wire Service. "Jacqueline Kennedy Onassis; 1929–1994." *St. Petersburg Times,* 20 May 1994, 1A.

Trewin, Ion. "Obituary: Jacqueline Kennedy Onassis." *The Independent,* 21 May 1994, 45.

Veness, Alison. "Jacqueline Kennedy Onassis: The First Lady of Fashion Set Her Own Style." *The Independent,* 21 May 1994, International 13.

Vespereny, Cynthia, and Bryna Taubman. "O, Camelot's." *New York Post,* 27 April 1996, 6.

Weber, Katharine. "Memoir: Antiquing with Jacqueline Onassis." *Architectural Digest,* May 1996, 56–62.